The Better of Goodman Ace

books by Goodman Ace

THE BETTER OF GOODMAN ACE
THE FINE ART OF HYPOCHONDRIA OR HOW ARE YOU?

GOODMAN ACE

The Better of
Goodman Ace

Doubleday & Company, Inc.
Garden City, New York, 1971

To My Typewriter
Which Has Kept Me in Touch

Contents

RATED X
Parents Not Admitted to This Section
Unless Accompanied by Children.

RX
Only Sick People Go to Doctors' Offices.

FLOTSAM
All I Don't Know Is What I Read in the Papers.

JETSAM
Old Age Is Wasted on the Elderly.

AND THENSOME
Consisting of Flotsam and Jetsam.

TV
Shorthand for Trivia.

GOD

. . . Is in His Heaven, and All Is Wrong with the World

Rated X

**Parents Not Admitted to this Section
Unless Accompanied by Children**

1.   SEX STORY

There's one question I've been hearing a lot in the last few years: "Why don't you write a novel or a play?"

Since I'm the one who's been asking myself the question, I always reply, "I'm going to. Just as soon as I get a few things out of the way."

But lately several people in the publishing and theatrical rackets have been asking when I'm going to write a novel or a play. Now I've changed my answer to: "Funny you should ask. I'm working on a novel right now, which I expect to adapt to a play."

If that answer doesn't make me sound important, at least it makes me sound industrious. Because actually, all I've done is to scribble some notes, and to outline a plot on the back of an envelope. (If it worked for him, why not for me?)

Well, it doesn't take long for a rumor like that to spread. It even reached the ears of the top, distinguished producer of Broadway plays who lives in our building. One day, in the elevator, he introduced himself and said, "I understand you have a play in mind."

"Yes, I have," I replied.

"I'd like to see it," he said.

"Thank you, sir. I'll send my mind down to your office next Monday," I answered.

I have this fascinating manner of ingratiating myself with people. He hasn't spoken to me since.

Of course, writing a novel would, for me, indeed be novel writing. The only books I've written to date were compilations of the stuff I had already written. And every book has been on the non-Best Seller list for more weeks than I care to count. I am now under the impression that the publishers of my books print a copy whenever somebody orders one.

It was obvious that it was time for a change. To get the feel of a novel, I read all the top sellers and was convinced that writing a novel in our current idiom would be a breeze. The trick, it appeared to me, was to write a book on one of the two best-selling subjects: (1) The making of a President, or (2) a virgin.

I chose (2). It would be a novel on a subject about which I knew very little because I had always been afraid to ask. But I gathered from the novels I had read that the secret three-letter word is "Sex." If sex is what book lovers want, I'll give it to them. After all, they gave it to me on my other books.

With a fresh new ribbon in my typewriter, I began. I had big erotic plans. In the first chapter the girl wore skirts so mini they left nothing to the imagination. As I continued writing, imagination soon turned to machination, and by the end of the chapter I was completely depleted and wound up three days in bed.

The doctor diagnosed it as a condition in which the

mind was unable to keep the dates the body made. A case of the eyes being bigger than I could stomach.

Refreshed, I was back at my beautiful typewriter with its new, fresh ribbon. I reread the first chapter and pondered whether a best-selling novel was my bag. Some writers have it, some don't. And I was not about to admit that I didn't have it. After all, the sex novel is nothing new. Elinor Glyn had it. And I would prove that I, too, have it.

Chapter two. I was typing along at a fast clip until I ran into a calamitous difficulty. Jeffry and Samantha were about ready to appear on a deserted beach for a moonlight swim in the nude, including the usual best-selling carnal episode.

I was prepared for a graphic description of that classic scene, without which no best-seller can succeed. These two beautiful people had just scampered out of the surf and were running laughingly across the sands, when Samantha stumbled and fell to the beach with Jeffry sprawling down beside her.

And wouldn't you know that this stupid typewriter, with its new, fresh ribbon, wrote, "Samantha rose and said, 'No, Jeff, no,' and ran off into the darkness."?

I didn't need a doctor to tell me this was a case of a writer's drawing on his personal, pitiful experiences. No sir. Nudity was not my forte. So I put my clothes back on and decided to cool it.

Shoemaker, stick to your last. Stop fooling around with barefoot girls. I not only don't have it, I'm not even with it. Back to collecting pieces that have appeared in the *Saturday Review*.

The title I chose, *The Better of Goodman Ace*, raised

some eyebrows and doubts at the publishers' office. They suggested a stronger title, but I wasn't going to leave myself open to the sneer of some browser in a bookshop, opening a book at random, reading one of the chapters, and saying, "Is that his best?" Nobody ever says, "Is that his better?"

Protection, see? Groovy!

2. OH, SAY CAN YOU SEE?

If I never see another thigh again as long as I live, it'll be all right with me. Is that what the girls have been hiding all these years? Big deal!

Skirts have come a far furlong up the skeletal ladder. And the girls have a ready answer. "What's the big deal? It's no more than you see when we're in swimming."

So, down Fifth Avenue they swim, using the potent back stroke, heads held mini-high, outwardly impervious to the stares, the whiplash crackling of male neck muscles, but inwardly delighted with being girls and with the excitement they radiate. Their spirits are raised higher than if they had been smoking "grass." Which in my day, I recall, was something you "keep off of the."

It was many years ago, I remember dimly, when a naughty girl clad in the long folds of her maidenly raiment permitted a phalange to peek. Then one day a fast woman showed a tarsus. Men began to rubberneck and nudge each other and say, "I love my wife, but oh you kid!"

Soon after, in 1920, Congress wrote an amendment to the Constitution declaring: "The right of citizens of the United States to vote shall not be denied or abridged by the United States or by any state on account of sex."

"Well," said the girls, "if that's what Congress wants!" So the flappers obliged by raising their skirts to exhibit a fibula. And the cake-eaters shouted in delight, "Bravo, bravo," and "Hear, hear."

The girls misunderstood "Hear, hear" for "Higher, higher." So skirts were obligingly heightened to show a fleeting peek of the patella. And for many years fashion fluctuated between fibula and a glimpse of the patella.

Men were afire. And girls began to smoke. "It's better than a smoker," said the boys, as if they were seated in what was known as the baldheaded row in a girlie show.

And the ladies played it to the hilt—the hilt having become several inches above the patella. And then for some seasons dropping one year to the fibula, then back up to a soupçon of patella again. Women sat before their spinning wheels, one evening lowering a hem, the next evening raising it.

And with each rising, men stood and saluted, and recited their pledge of allegiance to the unflagging energy of liberated women.

All this I accepted in good but bemused grace. Now it's the mini, and I walk behind girls who exhibit not only a popliteal fossa but plenty of femur. They are again playing to the boys, who these days cannot by any stretch of the imagination be considered the baldheaded row.

OK. Are you still with me? Don't get me wrong. I don't want you to think that I thought I could make you think that I'm not enjoying all this new freedom of peek. Then, you may ask, why was I plaintively saying that if I never see another thigh again it will be all right with me? I'll tell you why. I resent seeing the girls, in order to accommodate the miniskirts, shortening their mink coats. That's why.

Or any coat, for that matter. But mink particularly. A mink is a coat of fur that women have always dreamed of owning one day—luxurious in its enfolding length against the bitter cold of winter. A length that protects everything from ankle to leg to knee to thigh. And especially the popliteal fossa.

Shortening a mink coat is like cutting two inches off of a hundred-dollar bill because it doesn't fit into your new billfold. It's a sin. If God had wanted a mink coat to be short, He would have made a mink's pelt thigh length.

I've dwelt at some length—some pleasurable length I must add—on the esthetical; now for the practical. After months of all that dazzling display of feminine epidermis, shouldn't there be a three-month breather for the male? In the winter shouldn't all that curvature be contained under wraps? Even in a burlesque show there are comedy sketches between the take-it-off numbers.

Any actor will tell you that if he is seen too often as a guest on too many TV shows he will lose his welcome. And we all know that any woman who dons a mink automatically becomes an actress.

Taking a page from show biz, and in spite of the dictates of fashion, a woman bundled in a full-length mink to protect herself from the icy winds of zero weather and developing pneumonia from exposure, is also protecting herself against man's developing boredom with overexposure. 'Tis the season not to take-it-off, but to hide-it-away and come back in the spring with a whole new act.

Speaking of new acts, and assuming that art imitates life, the theater has taken a leaf from life—a fig leaf if you will, and has begun to go the miniskirt one better. You will be hard put to find an Off-Broadway play where nudity does not abound.

Many years ago, the sight of a chorus girl's knee was considered a shocker. In fact, one famous critic of the early thirties, reviewing a Broadway play, wrote: "The music is forgettable, the book is negligible, the scenery is deplorable, and the acting is lamentable. You may have noticed I have knocked everything but the chorus girls' knees, and God took care of that."

But the critics' sights are higher now, their reviews seldom dwell on nudity. Which is not the case with the New York Police Department. Recently an entire cast of a play was arrested down in old Greenwich Village. The charge was indecent exposure.

Eleven persons were dressed and taken into duress vile, including, the papers stated, a wardrobe mistress. She was unquestionably the least occupied member of any stage union.

Since then the police have given up being critics, and the Village features many such unclad plays. This is the Village which once upon an earlier and less liberated, though more enlightened, time, was the home of the experimental theater. This was where the prolific Eugene O'Neill once wrote what was, for that day, daring theater. Playwrights, finding Broadway less willing to produce meaningful plays, bared their souls and staged untried art forms.

But in the past few years, any young avant-garde man with a typewriter, and a vocabulary of four letter words (such as "free" and "love") has a go at a play. Having seen the glory of the buck in lines in front of the theaters where nudity prevails, he pounds out a play, and instead of baring his soul, he bares his cast.

Of course the girls will be appalled to learn that they are being held responsible for motivating all these theatrical sexhibitions. One young friend who hove into view wearing the most minuscule mini these eyes ever beheld, was disturbed by my evaluation of her garb.

"Oh, no," I said, "that's about the worst I've seen."

"I know," she said. "I shouldn't have bought it. It's the wrong color."

But I can't believe they're all that oblivious to their display. It's part of their act. As someone once said, "All the world's a stage and all the men and women merely players."

"They have their exits and their entrances; and one man in his time plays many parts."

Unfortunately, I get the feeling that on the program the part I'm playing is listed as "Peeping Tom." I didn't ask for the part, I was cast for it and I try to play it inoffensively. No leering, just wide-eyed wonder with just a touch of bewilderment.

I realize this treatise on the mini is an exercise in futility. No woman is going to lengthen anything—the miniskirt will still measure about two hands above the knee. And mink coats will follow upward and onward.

It isn't so bad when they're standing and walking. But when they sit, it's the fringe benefits that get me.

The question is: If they insist on exhibiting fibulae and patellae and popliteal fossae and femora, can acetabula be far behind?

3. THE DIRTY FIVE-LETTER WORD

Elke Sommer is an attractive movie actress. Recently she appeared on the *Merv Griffin Show* on CBS and asked people to write letters appealing for PEACE.

Carol Burnett is a gifted TV entertainer. She appeared on the *Merv Griffin Show* on Christmas Day and asked people to write letters appealing for PEACE.

Snip, snip. The CBS censors cut the appeals out of both programs.

Having survived and risen above the early days of censorship when "damn" and "hell" were snipped, television has now taken the giant step backward for all mankind. PEACE is a dirty word on all the talk shows. And the guests who appear on them are hereby warned to "watch it" when the subject comes up, if indeed it will ever again be permitted to come up.

"Talk shows" is a euphemism for "chatter shows." Too often the guests who show up on these midnight programs are hired at coolie wages to sit there making idle chatter while the host holds up—to plug—an author's unread book, or a singer's unheard album, or stills from an actor's unseen latest movie. This is not fair pay for the sleep a viewer loses.

If this censorship prevails—and the way everybody seems to be backing out of saying anything (I hate to use the word) meaningful, censorship will fast become the In thing. Dialogue on the chatter shows has been sinking into incredible banality. Censorship can only depress it further.

The sad part is that the lower the standard of dialogue, the higher the rating. For instance, the appearance of Mr. and Mrs. Tiny Tim on Johnny Carson's show. It is to the everlasting shame of our nation's viewers that when this quaint couple was married one midnight some time ago, in full view of millions of insomniacs, the program got its top rating. No censorship here. Marriage is in. Peace is out.

Of course, this was only a one-shot hypo for Mr. Carson. How often can Tiny Tim get married? What does he do for an encore? It's to the credit of Mr. Carson's restraint that he didn't order his cameras to accompany the couple on their honeymoon. Perhaps there is already in the works some sort of plan to bring them back to tell about it.

It would be a pleasant surprise if Mr. Tim did come back, a married and stable citizen, willing and anxious to discuss some of the problems that beset the world—and now him—such as the population explosion and planned parenthood.

"Would you want to discuss that?" Mr. Carson might ask, hopefully leading his victim into whatever disaster that might bring on.

"Of course, I want to talk about it," Mr. Tim might say. "I have the courage of my convictions. I have two lips to speak out, and I won't tiptoe through these two lips to speak my mind."

It would be the icing on the wedding cake, if he had read up on the subject and actually had (here I go again) something meaningful to say. Actually, it might be required by hosts of these shows that all guests bone up on a subject of some import. Instead of what I heard the other evening on David Frost's "talk" show.

Gig Young, actor, was a guest. He spent the first five or ten minutes reading off a cue card the names of the entire cast in his next movie. Then Mr. Frost, usually more astute, made the mistake of asking Gig Young if his real name is Gig Young. That sent Mr. Young into a complicated and desultory explanation of the time he made his first movie and played a character named Gig Young. So the producer who, I suppose, had tried to find a catchy name for his actor changed the billing to read "Gig Young played by Gig Young."

When I went to bed, I slept soundly after that information. I had turned and tossed through many a night wondering if Gig Young is really Gig Young's real name. Haven't you? Anyway, no censorship there. Gig Young is in. Peace is out.

How lucky we are there was no TV, or censor, when Matthew recorded the Sermon on the Mount. If he had been a guest on a late show to plug the Beatitudes, he would probably have run into some trouble.

"Blessed are the poor in spirit," he would have said, "for theirs is the kingdom of heaven.

"Blessed are the meek, for they shall inherit the earth.

"Blessed are the pure in heart, for they shall see God.

"Blessed are the peacemakers, for they shall be called the children of God."

Snip, snip.

4. WHAT'S A NICE GIRL LIKE YOU DOING IN A PLACE LIKE THIS?

If you were going to write a star-spangled piece for a July 4 weekend, and you decided to feature the Statue of Liberty, where would you go for your research? Whom would you call—*The New York Times*, the Public Library, or the New York Historical Society?

Not me. I phoned the Statue of Liberty. Oh, don't say that! She was in the Manhattan phone book, "Statue of Liberty, Lbrty Isl . . . RE 2-1286."

I phoned. If a man had answered, I was going to hang up. But no, she answered herself.

"Hello, Statue of Liberty?" I asked.

"Yes," a most pleasant voice replied.

"Oh," I said, groping for words, unaccustomed as I am to speaking to famous statues. "I'm uh—I was looking for some information for an article I'm doing. How do I get out there?"

"You take the ferry at the Battery to Liberty Island. Or, as it is known, to Bedloe's Island."

"Thank you. I'll be seeing you, Miss. That's a date now." "Fresh," she said, and slammed her receiver.

Not a very propitious start for an interview, but being the devil-may-care reporter I am, I took out my hat that said PRESS, set it at a rakish angle, and went to interview the Lady in the Harbor. She wasn't too enthused.

"I don't give interviews to everybody," she said. "You should have phoned for an appointment."

"I did. You told me how to get here."

"Oh, that's one of my secretaries. That's my listed number. I had to put in an unlisted phone. All those immigrants calling up. They came here looking for streets paved with gold, and hope for a new freedom and a life of tranquillity—crank calls, complaining."

"Well, I see it says down here: 'Give me your tired, your poor. Your huddled masses yearning to breathe free. . . .'"

"Yearning to breathe free—in this polluted air?" she scoffed.

"'The wretched refuse of your teeming shore. Send these, the homeless, the tempest-tost to me. . . .'"

"I know what it says," she interrupted. "Of course, I can't read it from up here. But everybody who comes out here feels called upon to recite it. And out loud! Gets tiresome after eighty-three years."

"Eighty-three years old," I said, making a note.

"Watch your language, Buster. I don't like the way you put it. But you can say this girl has been carrying the torch for eighty-three years. That's a little joke I put in all my interviews."

"Thank you, that'll spice it up."

"Oh, if that's the kind of paper you're writing for, you can also say that I don't pay my own light bill for this torch."

"You mean—are you implying—?"

"Draw your own inferences. That was all taken care of back in 1886 when old Grover Cleveland turned me on."

"Old Grover Cleveland turned you on?" I asked, writing furiously.

"Yeh, how about that!"

"I'm not surprised. You are attractive. May I ask what you weigh?"

"I weigh 450,000 pounds. But I have the height for it, don't you think?"

"Oh sure, a nice figure of a girl."

"My waist is twenty-five."

"Twenty-five feet," I wrote.

"Hold it," she said. "What are you, a troublemaker? Just let it go at a twenty-five waist. Oh, excuse me, here comes another ship. I have to play hostess again. Oh, it's the *S. S. France*. Got to be especially gracious; they sent me over here, you know. In 214 packing cases! Talk about going steerage! Bless their little hearts, they're waving. *Bonjour, mes amis! Bonjour! Comment allez-vous? Bonjour! Bon appétit* at '21' Club!"

"'21' Club? What's that about?"

"Oh, that. I throw in a commercial to make them think I'm sponsored. You don't get a prime-time audience without a sponsor, especially since I'm only a documentary."

"But why wish them *bon appétit?* It's the poor and hungry and tempest-tost immigrants you're supposed to welcome to our shores for a life of peace and tranquillity."

"It's a bitter joke, isn't it," she said softly, "what with all the poor and hungry and tempest-tost who are already on our shores? If something isn't done about them quickly, instead of holding this flame to welcome immigrants, I'll be using my hand to wave good-bye to emigrants sailing off to find tranquillity somewhere else."

"Where on earth could that be?"

"Not on earth. Haven't you heard? They've given up on tranquillity on earth. Next, the moon—I hear there's a whole sea of it up there."

5. MOVIES GO FROM BED TO WORSE

If you were in New York City last month and you wanted to see the movie *Lady In Cement,* and you had phoned the theater, as I did, to find out when the picture went on, you would have heard what I heard. It took three calls to be able to jot it down like it was:

"For our colored feature," the disembodied voice said, "persons under 16 will not be admitted unless accompanied by parent or adult party. This is a recording announcement from Cinema 57 Rendezvous. We are located on 57th Street just west of Sixth Avenue. We are easy to reach by all subways and by bus. Our feature is *Lady In Cement.* Our stars are Frank Sinatra as tough Tony Rome, Raquel Welch, a girl with a 37-22-35 measurement, and Big Dan Blocker of TV *Bonanza* fame. Miami is the scene, with killers and cops and topless bikinis."

Following this graphic hard sell, there was the schedule of the day's showings, which ended with: "For further information please dial Judson 6-4449. Thank you for calling."

Well, I needed further information on the vital statistics. This time a live woman answered.

"Hello," I said, "is this Cinema 37?"

"No, this is Cinema 57," she replied.

"Oh? But I just listened to your recording, and it said 37."

"Oh, well that must be a mistake. We'll have to look into—are you interested in seeing Frank Sinatra?"

"Usually. But not at a time like this."

"Oh, we have later time schedules."

"Thank you. And that's 37th Street, you say?"

"Yes. No! It's 57th Street!"

"Oh yes, thanks very much."

Let's say I'm a boy of 14, and I have called the movie house and heard that recording. That evening after dinner I have decided I need an adult or a parent. I choose a parent.

"Dad," I say, "you promised if I got good marks you'd take me to a movie. I got good marks. How about taking me to see *Lady In Cement?*"

"What kind of a picture is that?" Dad asks warily.

"It's about killers and cops."

"Oh no. You're not going to see a picture that's all about shooting and killing."

"It can't be *all* about that. Because there's a little girl in it who is 37 inches tall. She must be his little daughter."

"Thirty-seven inches? A child? Who told you that?"

"I called the movie house, and the record told me."

"Well, I'll see about that. I'll call up and see."

Dad dials the number and listens:

"Yes . . . hm hm . . . yes . . . yes . . . YEH? . . . No kidding!"

He hangs up and dials again.

"Who you calling now, Dad?"

"I want to get further information. Hello, is this Cinema 37?"

"No, this is Cinema 57. This is the second call I've had today about that. I checked it. The record says Cinema 57. Raquel is 37."

"Thank you." Dad hangs up. "Well, son, if your mind is set on seeing that movie, I'll take you. But let's not tell Mom, OK?"

What is happening here is a self-imposed censorship by the motion picture industry. There seem to be three parts to this voluntary moral code, and they are so indicated in the newspaper ads:

1) "Persons under 16 not admitted." These are the obviously smutty Sex Films.

2) "Persons under 16 not admitted unless accompanied by a parent or an adult." These are the Normal Sex Films plus messy Violence.

3) "Suggested for General Audiences." These are the tidy old Bessie Love and Billie Dove films all the way.

Some of the ads leave it to your own judgment and conscience by quoting the movie critics: "Fun and Games Mother Never Taught," says one critic. Another: "Makes Virginia Woolf Look Like Little Women." Or one movie owner who became his own critic: "See Barbarella Do Her Thing All Over New York."

There is one movie from Sweden, "I Am Curious—Yellow," which was shelved after a Federal Court jury

of seven men and five women voted the film was obscene. However, in the Appeals Court the judges voted
that it was not obscene, in spite of the jury's findings that
the film displayed the sex content "with greater explicit-
ness than any movie thus far exhibited in this country."

It is not too unreasonable to imagine when that picture
is released, the ads will say, "Only Persons Will Be Admitted Who Do Not Believe the Stork Story."

6. THE MIDI SKIRT AND THE FEMINIST MOVEMENT

The rise of the New Feminism and the plunge of the miniskirt, both of which have made the current scene simultaneously, are not coincidental. Worse yet, in combination they form an obvious contradiction.

Let's take it from the beginning. The very beginning. In the beginning, you remember, God created the Heaven and the Earth, and a paradise known as the Garden of Eden. And when He turned on the light, He saw that it was good. (You can't do better research than the Bible—the old and unrevised version.)

There was this lonesome man in the garden. So, just for a rib, God gave him a woman. "And they were both naked," says Genesis 2:25, "the man and his wife, and were not ashamed."

He told them they could eat freely the fruits from all the trees in the garden, save one. That was the apple tree, the tree of knowledge. Also in the garden was this serpent, "more subtile than any beast in the field."

The serpent told the woman it was Green and Go on

the apple tree. "Apples are not all that knowledgeable. Apples only know how to keep the doctor away," said the serpent.

"Serpent," she replied, "you speak with forked tongue. We have been told the apples are a no-no."

"Take a bite," the snake hissed.

And she did, and her eyes "were opened," and she "knew" that she was "naked." So she put a hem on a fig leaf and placed it strategically to hide her nudity. That pasty was the first mini.

But when God saw what she had done, He was outraged. He evicted her and her husband from the garden. No more fruit trees. He sent them east of Eden into the field. "Thistles and thorns shall it bring forth to thee; and thou shalt eat the herb of the field."

Bitter punishment! But it can be easily deduced that in the beginning, the very beginning, God favored nudity. And if so much wrath was wrought over a single fig leaf to hide nakedness, it is easy to imagine the heavenly turmoil that must have been created by the coming into fashion of the midi to hide a couple of knees.

The Bible has a way of repeating itself. In the beginning there was the mini in our Garden of Eden. There was also this famed fashion designer, Serpentino, who spoke to the woman, saying unto her, "The midi is in. If you wear a mini you just don't know your apples." So she changed to midi.

This is the same woman who, only a spring ago, came home to model for her husband her newest mini.

"Haw!" he exclaimed. "It's too short."

"Don't you haw at my hem," she replied tartly. "And don't be a square."

A fashion designer, you see, is round. And rich. And getting four times richer with the coming of every season.

This cavalier attitude toward second-class citizens known as husbands is inflammatory Feminism. But when some strange, designing man tells her that her hemline should be below her knees, she is off on a shopping spree to fulfill his chameleonic whims. That's barefaced Femininism, new and old! Go figure.

But hold! There is hope. There is another serpent in our Garden of Eden. This one is a good serpent. Revlon. In a full-page ad announcing the new "Midi Look Face," and displaying a raft of cosmetics, it asks in bold type this question: WHEN LEG WATCHERS TURN INTO FACE WATCHERS, WILL YOU BE READY FOR THEM TO WATCH YOU?

By heaven, hoisted by their own petard! Trouble in the Garden of Eden! And what a time for some enterprising fashion designer to come out with a whole set of new minis and a new advertising campaign: TO BE WORN ONLY BY WOMEN WITH BEAUTIFUL LEGS.

Where now the Feminist who will hide hers under a midi for all the world to know that she hasn't?

7. PORNOGRAPHER'S COMPLAINT

As the new theatrical season opens on Broadway, the big hit is Off-Broadway, where *Oh! Calcutta!* is packing them in skintight. This brand nude production is the work of several renowned writers who contributed the pornographic sketches that everybody's talking about, but few ever confess to having seen.

Since the musical *Hair* opened on Broadway with five or six unclothed actors standing still onstage, nudity has become the acceptable eighth lively art, and nobody breaks down any doors. But when the art gets too lively—instant hit. Which *Oh! Calcutta!* is. Even those exclamation marks look lascivious!

Gordon Crowe, associate producer of *Oh! Calcutta!* offered me two free seats for opening night. "No sir!" I said. "I wouldn't walk across the street to see a degrading, immoral, shameless sexhibition like that."

"How do you know?" he asked. "You haven't seen it."

"Oh no? Did I ever tell you about this recurring dream I have? And I have another complaint, my real com-

plaint. How come you, a producer, my friend, brother
Friar, didn't ask me to contribute a sketch?"

"I didn't know you could write stuff like that."

"Are you mad?" I shouted. "When I was ten years old
I used to write stuff like that on fences."

Next case: A letter from Jill Goldstein, associate editor
of *Esquire*, "Dear Mr. Ace: *Esquire* is currently planning
a special December issue in which we will have a major
feature exploring sexual candor and nudity in the arts.
. . . Perhaps you might want to participate in the feature,
which will include a group photograph of notable people
from many fields of endeavor . . . posed and lighted in a
manner similar to the attached Photostat. The partici-
pants, of course, would be nude."

Attached was a Photostat of a nude young fellow
three-quarters profile, his hands strategically placed.

My immediate reaction was a shudder. In a December
issue of *Esquire*, me on the newsstands freezing my hands
off? Thanks, not me, Jill.

Then I decided to sleep on it. It was no go. If I said
"yes," would Jill lose respect for me? Would she think I
was fast, an easy nude? Does she kiss and tell; had I been
first on her list (alphabetically); had all the others turned
her down; was it the old Saturday night without a date
bit?

I didn't have long to wait for the answer. Before a
week was out, I read that Cleveland Amory had been
asked. And later, in *The New York Times* another notable,
Ned Rorem, wrote that he too had been accosted by Jill.

Well, wouldn't you say I had a right to feel jilted? But
through my tears, I was glad I found out in time, glad do
you hear me? I wrote demanding to know what kind of a

fellow she thought I was. She didn't think I was much of a fellow. She didn't answer. Cad!

However, again that wasn't my real complaint. In the July issue, *Esquire* asked fifty notables to contribute what they thought the first man on the moon should say. Again, I wasn't asked to contribute. Surrounded by assassins! Jill only thinks of me as a nude model. A fellow likes to believe a girl admires him for his mind too, you know.

When I finished reading the *Esquire* moon quotes, I was glad, do you hear me, glad, I hadn't been asked. The cover showed famous men in earlier historic days, along with quotes they were purported to have made at the time of their greatness. I couldn't believe any of them.

Especially the one by Alexander Graham Bell, and what *Esquire* reports he said into the first telephone: "Watson, come here, I need you."

Poppycock! If there were ever a man who didn't need Watson any more, Bell was that man. He probably said, "Beat it, Watson, the invention works, thanks a lot, pick up your check, see you around some time, don't call me, I'll call you, if you ever get a phone."

As for the quote by the first man on the moon, I had a line for him with which Jill would have scooped the world.

On that unbelievable day when a man first set foot on the moon, and stared in awe at the moonscape of that stark coil of uncharted void, there was only one natural thing he would say—"Take me to your Liederkranz."

But he didn't, and history books, alas, will never record it. All because Jill was too busy trying to maneuver me into her plush, dimly lit, softly cushioned photography studio to see her etchings.

8. QUESTIONING THE SKIRT

When the miniskirt was invented and the first one came chug-chugging down the street, I was one of the guys who stood on the sidewalk shouting, "Get a horse." Things looked bad for the morals of our generation.

But in surprisingly little time, the mini became acceptable, part of the scenery—like a tree that wears a nest of robins in her hair. And we all know that only God can make a woman.

Then things really began looking up. The miniskirt soon became the minuscule. And when a girl in a minuscule skirt came marilynmonroeing down the avenue, the guys said, "Disgusting." As they wiped clear their steamed-up glasses. And this tiny, abbreviated skirt soon became acceptable, part of the scenery—like a tree that wears a nest of robins in her hair. And nothing else. And when that girl in a minuscule skirt merely sat down to play the piano, they all applauded.

There is no gainsaying—if you can tolerate a little old-fashioned no-gain-saying philosophy—that the miniskirt

liberated women and gave them a new found freedom
of motion and expression.

The girls thrived on all that applause and on the re-
peated cries of "Brava, brava." Standing centerstage in
a spotlight, they took encore after encore. It was heady
stuff, like drinking champagne from a slipper.

However, as it often happens in show biz, the girls began to believe their rave reviews. They organized. They
demanded better billing. Equal billing with men. They
were tired of being thought of as manikins in salons.
They demanded entrance into saloons. They got it. They
even went on strike, and paraded down Fifth Avenue,
striking while the iron was cold.

Strangely enough, the men still shouted and applauded.
There was gaiety and abandon in the air. It was as if we
were all players in an erotic Off-Broadway production,
set on the sands of an exotic seaside beach.

But, alas, the curtain is about to descend. It's a maxi
curtain, a mid-calf midi curtain, a nonasbestos curtain.
The fire has gone out. If Fashion has its way—and department store ads indicate it will—the mini is out.
Women will no longer be clothed, they will be cloaked
from mandibula to tarsus, and from fore to aft.

The midi and the maxi will henceforth cover a multitude of shins. And one asks, "Why?" The bare look can't
be blamed for inflation, it didn't touch off the campus
riots or high interest rates, it didn't bankrupt the Penn
Central Railroad, and it didn't start the war in Indo-
china.

No sooner have we become accustomed to the bare
look, taken it in stride, than we are suddenly told we shall
see no more legs. Too bad. Even our Vice President

would never admit that when you've seen one pair of
legs you've seen them all.

Then, why? I'll tell you why. Because some French
couturier by the name of Jacques Farine, whose family
had been for a hundred years in the flour sack business,
decided to stuff a woman into a new fashion. So that he
could make more money? Partly, maybe.

But he had a more insidious motive. He hated women
—especially liberated women. He would take away their
act by covering them with yards of material.

I went to see Monsieur Farine, and he said, "Look
at beautiful, exquisite Juliet. She wore long-flowing robes.
A lot of material was there. And she was all woman."

"Yes," I replied, "and look what happened to her! And
to Cleopatra, and to Lady Macbeth. But you take Peter
Pan, plenty of legs and thighs showing there. Everyone
could see that Peter Pan had a beautiful figure like Mary
Martin. No more legs on the streets would be enough
to drive us all back into those sex-movie theaters. And
besides, every woman sweeping down the street in a
maxi dress will become her own Sanitation Department."

"*Fausse. Au contraire.* Every woman in a maxi dress
will wear it nobly and with dignity. You will see."

"You're just doing this because down deep you really
hate women."

"*Au contraire!* You are wrong. I have worked very hard
to become the great couturier that I am. I was poor, working with my family in the mills, until I came to Paris.
Good fortune was mine, until the miniskirt. Then my
fortune dwindled. Now I am once again back where I
started."

"Yes, in the flour sack business."

We parted bad friends. He was as wrong as all but fifty million Frenchmen can be. However, the maxi or the mini or the midi—it's only academic. With all this air pollution, who can see anything anyway?

RX

Only Sick People
Go to Doctors' Offices

9. OPEN YOUR EYES AND SAY "AH"

Did I tell you about this trouble I have in movie houses? I think I did, but I'd like you to hear it again. I'm farsighted and I don't hear too well. So when I go to the flicks, I have to sit far back to see and up close to hear. That keeps me pretty busy running up and down the aisle to make out what's happening on the screen. I was once picked up in a small movie theater for molesting— but that's another story.

What reminded me of my condition was this letter I have from J. Bruce Guyselman of Albion, Michigan. He writes about his glasses: "I finally convinced my optician that my right lens needed a rotation. If I closed my left eye and twisted the frame, I got a dandy view with my right eye. The optician seemed impressed by this demonstration. But, alas, do you know how many different shapes and sizes of lenses there are? I'll guess 1,648 in honor of the French victory at Lens. A new glass was finally ground. I knew it was perfect because the view got fuzzy when I twisted the frame."

I recognize the scene, Mr. G. The last time I saw my optician, it was not too clearly. He went through the usual routine, sat me facing the chart and said, "Read that top line." I recited it.

"No, no," he said, "don't look at me. Look at the chart and read it."

"Aw, Doctor, it's the same chart you've had for years. I know what it says."

"You're being difficult," he informed me. "What trouble do you seem to be having?"

"Seeing."

"Is that seeing reading, or seeing seeing?"

"Beg pardon?"

"Do you have trouble seeing up close or at a distance?"

"Well, I was in St. Louis recently and I couldn't see there either . . . . Well, Doctor? . . . Doctor?"

"Oh, yes. St. Louis. Now, which eye bothers you most?"

"I think that should be 'more,' since there are only two, except when I wear these glasses which make it four. And that's what I want to ask you about—these glasses. My right eye doesn't recognize what my left eye is reading. Like the other day I was reading the morning paper and there was this quote from a prominent national politician who said, 'We cannot sit down to negotiate peace until we have as many missiles than Russia has.'"

"As many *than* Russia has?"

"That's what I read. Of course, my left eye correctly recognized it as a Freudian slip, but my right eye saw it as a case of a man's not knowing his *than* from his *as*. Which, you'll admit, was a pretty jaundiced view of it. Where are you going, Doctor?"

"I'm just going to sit down here. Go on."

"Well, that's my hangup. While shaving, I've spoken pretty sharply to both my eyes. I've told them it's a complex world, beset by many problems, and they have to learn to live together and to communicate, or WW III will break out in my head, I told them."

"And what did your eyes say?"

"Well, my eyes are not too expressive. The left eye showed a gleam of understanding. But my right eye—the militant eye—it was for protests and demonstrations."

"Very interesting. They don't see eye to eye."

"Hey, that was clever, Doc."

"Oh, it was nothing."

"Exactly. Now do you have a cure for this sort of thing?"

"Well, if you're asking me to cure the world's ills, I wish I could."

"No, let's get back to my eyes."

"No, I like this comparison of your eyes to the ugly Weltschmerz we are experiencing today."

"You mean ugliness is in the eye of the beholder?"

"Beautiful! Yes, that's it. I can use that in an article I have to write next month for the *Myopic World* magazine. I'll make a note of it. Where are my glasses?"

"On top of your head. But Doctor, why I really came here was to have my eyes examined. That's it—look into them."

"Yes, I am. Eyes are beautiful."

"Later, Doctor."

"As du Bartas said it in the sixteenth century: 'These lovely lamps, these windows of the soul.'"

"Du Bartas? I heard it was that most famous astigmat-

ic of them all, Dr. Milton Reder. He said it in Club 21:
'The eyes are the windows of the soul.' But do you really
believe that window stuff, Doctor?"

"It is the creed of my profession."

"OK. Then give me a prescription for a bottle of Win-
dex and a squeegee."

"That'll be $20."

I paid him with two tens. Which is my vision in each
eye.

10. SOMBERLY

As it must to everyone, it fell to my lot some months ago
to be appointed, for the first time, the "arranger" of a funeral. A close and cherished member of the family had
died.

He had not passed on, or passed over, or departed,
or left us. He died. Years before his span. Suddenly.

The shock absorbed, replaced by the usual and unreasonable bitterness and the asking of why, I entered the
funeral parlor. Black-suited, black-tied attendants directed me softly to the man in charge of such details. He
sat behind a desk spotlessly clean of all clutter. I resented
him for that. But I realized here was a man who knew
where everything, and everybody, belonged.

"This won't take long, will it?" I asked.

"No," he replied, drawing a long printed form from
his desk, "only about thirty minutes." An eternity.

With pen poised, he asked the first startling question.
"What was his Social Security number?"

I shook my head. He could see I didn't know. He could

also see how inept an arranger I was going to be. Other questions followed, and he was helpful in leading me to answers. I don't remember all the questions, but I have total recall of the last four:

"Now what about flowers?" he asked.

"We have asked that flowers be omitted," I replied.

"No, I mean the spray on the casket. Do you want a spray?"

"Well, I guess so."

"They come in three sizes. There's the small piece placed in the center, or the three-quarter length, or the blanket of flowers that covers the entire casket."

"Well, I don't know. What would you think?"

"May I suggest the three-quarter length?"

I nodded.

He made the entry as he said, "Flowers, seventy-nine dollars. Now, what about music? Something classical?"

"I suppose so."

"Bach? Beethoven? Mozart?"

"Yes," I replied, as I felt myself disintegrating.

"Which one?"

"I don't know," I said rising, unreasonably disturbed at my own inadequacy to answer a few simple questions.

As I paced, he remained calm and made a note on the form, and asked the next question.

"Now, what about clothes?"

I sat again in utter bewilderment. This was to be a cremation. Did it matter? I gathered it did from his next remark.

"We can furnish a suit, if you like. Or some prefer a robe or even pajamas."

He waited for my answer while I sat there thinking, "This too shall pass." But it didn't.

"I suggest pajamas," he offered.

I nodded.

He wrote, as he said, "Pajamas, twelve dollars and sixty cents." And then he added, "That includes the sales tax."

And there you have it—the two irrevocables, death and taxes.

As I was about to leave, he asked the fourth question, almost in passing. "By the way," he said, "have you signed the paper for the release of the deceased from the hospital?"

I hadn't. He said I should. He was right. All my other arrangements would have been rather flat without it.

He was quite helpful here. He phoned the hospital to tell them I was coming down to sign. Then he wrote down the window number and the name of the doctor I was to ask for.

When I arrived at the hospital, the doctor I was to see was out to lunch. There was some scurrying around to find him, and finally I was rescued by a courteous young man in an office who benevolently suggested that I sign the paper and he would have the doctor fill out the details later. I signed.

"I will mail you a copy," he said.

I thanked him for his help.

"Glad to be of service," he replied. He put out his hand, "Good-by, and I hope the next time we meet it will be under more pleasant circumstances." We shook on it.

In the cab on the way back I thought that over. "The next time we meet?" When? Where? When were we go-

ing to meet again? Socially? Hardly. Did he mean as a
bereaved or as a client?

A day to remember. Thinking back on it, I have the
feeling that the man for whom I made the arrangements
would have laughed at my discomfiture and joined with
me in my disapprobation of this "civilized" ritual.

What it amounts to is we go into a funeral shop to buy
a man something he wouldn't get for himself, and which
he has never had before.

11. A WRITER WHO MAKES HOUSE CALLS

Professional writing has a built-in occupational hazard. Hardly a week goes by that some non-writer doesn't call to ask me to write a routine he fancies he can deliver at a wedding, or a birthday, or a coming-out, or a going-into-retirement party.

"Only about a ten or a fifteen minute monologue," they say. "You can write that in five minutes."

Little does the caller know that on my portable I couldn't possibly. I was euchred into buying this puny typewriter by a man who kept saying: "Lift it. It's lighter than air." And it is. But he didn't mention it was so light that every time I push the carriage over for the next line, the thing flies off the desk, and I'm constantly on my toes to get to the bathroom before it does.

One such request came recently from my doctor after two horrendous days in his antiseptic office, during which I had my annual check-up, the whole bit—cardiogram, blood pressure, X-rays, encephalogram, and all those messy things that delight the doctor, so he can fill that mad array of little tubes and bottles and flasks he has lying around.

After he had run out of things for me to do, and I had run out of things with which to do them, I was invited into his office for consultation. He suggested I was working too hard. "Maybe you ought to take it easier," he said.

I had suggested this very proposition to the principal beneficiary of my life insurance policies and she had said, "You can't do that. There's an old saying: 'If you rest you rust.'"

So I said to the doctor, "I can't do that. There's an old saying 'If you rest you rust.' "

"Who said that?" the doctor asked.

"I don't know. I think it was Damocles."

"No," said the doctor, "he was the one with the sword. You're thinking of Democritus."

"Oh no. I remember him. He was that laughing Greek philosopher. How about Diogenes?"

"The old man with the lamp? No, no. You must mean Demosthenes, the fellow who put the pebbles in his mouth."

"That's the one who said it. The fellow with rocks in his mouth."

"Back to business," said this disciple of Hippocrates (or was it Hippomenes?). "I think I'll start a new card on you."

After some twenty years, he had compiled a huge dossier of yellowed and frayed cards on my various declining case histories. Now he pulled a spanking white piece of cardboard out of his desk. I was quick to notice that the new card was about two inches longer than the old

ones. It was the only hopeful sign I had detected during
the entire check-up.

Two weeks later, I received his astronomical bill, along
with a short note in his own handwriting.

"You are fit as a fiddle," the note began. If he had in
mind Jack Benny's fiddle, I was in big trouble. It probably
accounted for the buzzing I had been constantly trying
to brush away from my ears.

The note went on: "By the way, I have to attend a PTA
meeting next Thursday night. In your spare time, would
you mind knocking off a ten-minute monologue I can
deliver there? Make it funny because my daughter expects me to be quite amusing. It'll only take you a few
minutes. Have lunch with me so we can discuss this."

After cooling down, I accepted the luncheon invitation. He ordered two drinks, a cheeseburger with French
fries and pickles—all the things he had cautioned me not
to eat. While we waited for the lunch to be served, I
made my first pitch.

"Doctor," I said, "would you mind feeling my pulse?
It's unusually rapid today."

He felt it. And without looking at his watch he announced: "It feels all right to me."

"You sure?" I asked. "I know my heart is pounding.
Would you put your stethoscope to my chest and give
it a listen?"

"Stethoscope? Who's got a stethoscope? It's in my bag
in the car."

"Didn't you bring anything with you—your cardio-
graph machine—oxygen tent—how about an aspirin?"

"Come to my office if you want to be examined."

"Well, I thought as long as we're waiting for—"

"One doesn't practice medicine in his spare time. How unprofessional can you get? This is a social visit. Now about this monologue you're going to write for me. . . ."

Just as the check came he remembered a house call he had to make. What it was was he had to call *his* house. His wife worries that he forgets to eat lunch. Another thing the good doctor forgets is that writing can also be a profession.

12. MAN'S REAL BEST FRIEND

If you manage to survive the next thirty years and slip into the twenty-first century, whom will you have to thank for it? Not your dog. Full credit should go to your neighborhood mouse.

I know this dissertation is not going to make me any friends, but history will substantiate the premise. I too was once a dog lover. But let's consider the mouse. When modern science is on the verge of a break-through that will help to sustain and prolong life for mankind, who comes forward to test the new discovery? The mouse.

When a scientist called for volunteers to help stamp out poliomyelitis, who came scampering to the side of Dr. Jonas Salk? Not your dog—mice. While your dog was in the parlor, sitting up, or playing dead, or fetching a slipper, the mice were busy at their labs, selflessly and unstintingly donating their time, and baring their forearms to help test the efficacy of this new serum.

The story of how the mice got into the business of saving humanity from these dread scourges is worth the telling. The high position they have attained had a lowly beginning. It was back in the thirteenth century that a certain pied piper piped all the mice out of beautiful downtown Hamelin.

Having been driven from the lush, green countryside of Westphalia into the overcrowded urban areas, the mice were unable to find a peaceful haven. Wherever they set up homes, the fashionable inhabitants began moving out of the neighborhood, leaving the mice to forage in people-infested slums. They realized that something had to be done to raise their public image.

At first they tried to ingratiate themselves with acts of kindness. One mouse, for instance, pulled a thorn out of a lion's paw. This charitable act helped him but not all mousekind. And when people began inciting their cats to destroy them, the frustration of the mice turned to bitterness and finally to revolt against the Establishment.

They began to beat a path to the very doors of their persecutors. They squealed noisily through parlors and made terrified, shrieking women jump to safety on chairs. They gnawed at ships to make them sink, and as the crew went down, the mice laughingly deserted. Their favorite demonstration, according to an early chronicler named Hickory Dickory Dock, was to run up a clock and make it strike 1, no matter what the time.

All to no avail. Their best-laid schemes went aft agley. For 300 years they remained at the nadir of the social ladder.

But it was in the sixteenth century that they got their lucky break. It was almost like a fairy tale. There was this girl named Cinderella, a drudge, ragged and dirty from doing all the housework while her elder sisters were al-

ways on the town, going to dances, and meeting people
in high society.

Finally a good fairy enabled Cinderella to go to the
prince's ball by bedecking her in a dazzling gown with
slippers of glass and turning a pumpkin into a coach. And
who do you think was drawing the coach? A team of six
mice!

What a furor they created, prancing and high-stepping
their way to the prince's palace! The townsfolk who lined
the streets had seen coaches, dazzling gowns, and even
glass slippers before, but never a team of mice in such re-
splendent royal livery, worthy of a Disney. As the on-
lookers shouted and applauded, the mice knew they had
finally made it.

But their joy was short-lived. At midnight, as we all
know, the coach was turned back into a pumpkin, and
the mice disappeared back into the oblivion of their
holes. And there they remained for 400 years, unwanted
and untended. They wondered where is He Who sees
with equal eye a hero perish or a sparrow fall?

Which brings us to the enlightened twentieth century.
Now who is it who martyrs himself to help erase the in-
firmities of fragile man? You know who—thousands upon
thousands of our little friends, in spanking white, starched
hospital gowns, at the elbows of our researchers, eating,
drinking, and smoking so that man can enjoy a longer
life span.

It wasn't an easy decision for the mice, giving their
lives to a cause. But the silent majority prevailed in the
interest of their future progenies. There were of course
the usual dissidents who held out. They were regarded
as the effete snobs, the rat finks. But even they finally

joined the revolt when they heard they could apply for testing some of the hallucinatory drugs.

Now you know who your real best friend is. So watch it. Be a Big Brother. Take a mouse to lunch.

13. DID HIPPOCRATES START LIKE THIS?

My doctor is an outstanding, outspoken, outrageously dedicated man of medicine. But not outgoing. He makes no house calls after 9 p.m., when I'm always at death's door.

That was the hour I called him the other evening. His normally big, resounding voice answered with a scarcely audible croak of a "Hello."

"Is that you, doc? What's the trouble?"

"Oh, it's you," he whispered, "I think I'm fighting a virus. I had gone to sleep to ward it off."

"Oh, that's too bad, doc. I was calling to invite you and your wife to come to dinner tomorrow."

It turned out I was just what the doctor needed: a miracle cure.

"Tomorrow night?" he shouted. "Swell, we'll be there. Thanks."

If that Camille bit my doctor acts out doesn't tell it how it is with some doctors who don't make night calls, try this story. A woman phones her doctor at midnight. His wife answers.

"Oh, the doctor went out on an emergency call, Mrs. Harris. I don't know when he'll be back. What's the trouble?"

"It's my back. It's acting up again. I need the doctor right away."

"Oh," says the wife. "Well, uh . . ."

There is a hastily whispered consultation with the doctor, who, with his wife, has been lying there watching the *Johnny Carson Show*.

"Hello, Mrs. Harris," says his wife, "why don't you take two aspirins? That'll stop the pain."

"I already did that. It still hurts."

"Oh, you took the aspirin and it still hurts? Well, uh —(whispered consultation)—get into a hot bath."

"I did that. It doesn't help either."

"Oh, you took a hot bath and it didn't help? Well, uh— try dry heat. Do you have an electric pad?"

"Yes. I'll try that. Thank you. Oh, before I do that, tell me, is that man lying with you there also a doctor?"

That, unfortunately, is the way it is with a man dedicated to health. His health. The 9 p.m. air is not good for my doctor. And if on occasion he does venture into it, the box-office prices change to include his diagnosis, two taxi rides, treatment for the mugging he foresees, and the money he could have been robbed of.

A far cry from kindly old Doctor Herman Boerhaave of Holland (1668-1738). How I happened to know about kindly old Doctor Boerhaave is that I read about him when he was the cover boy on the December 1968 issue of the *Journal of the American Medical Association*, commemorating the 300th anniversary of his birth.

In the attendant article, G. A. Lindeboom, M.D.,

writes that Dr. Boerhaave at the age of sixteen had "graduated in philosophy after defending a thesis on the dis-
tinction between mind and body . . . then turned to
medicine with the intention, however, of taking care of
both souls and bodies simultaneously."

You can be sure that foremost diagnostician of his day,
philosopher, and teacher was never on the phone after
9 p.m. telling a patient to take nose drops for his sinus
and two aspirins for his soul, never mind that they didn't
have phones or nose drops in 1700.

Read carefully, if you will, Dr. Boerhaave's gentle diagnosis and prescription when called in for consultation
on a case of asthmatic bronchitis:

> It is to be feared that by the gentleman's staying so long
> in the cold water (which circumstance should have been
> first mentioned in the description) the *Nerves* belonging to
> the *Diaphragm* have been hurt, and hence so has the *Asthma*.
> This disorder is difficult of cure, which is very plain from
> this consideration, that so strong remedies as those already
> tryed, have done little or no service.
>
> I think the gentleman should try what the exercise of rid-
> ing might do; but then it must be pretty violent daily and
> long continued. I am confident it would be of service, and
> must recommend it as the principal remedy in this case. In
> the meantime we must join to it what is proper for the
> *Nerves*. Let him then every three hours, swallow three of
> the pills *A*, drinking immediately after them two ounces of
> the mixture *B*. I expect great benefit from this course if
> continued in for three months, and pray God may bless it.
> Signed H. B.

The other night I forgot to "close cover before striking," and so burned two fingers, a disorder difficult of

cure. Such was the pain to the *Nerves* belonging to my *Right Hand,* that hence I had the *Shakes,* and so spent a sleepless night. Although my doctor had suggested a tryed and true remedy, it had done little or no service, obviously because he had not called upon *Anyone* to bless the *Unguentine* which he had prescribed on the phone after 9 p.m.

14. NEEDLING THE DOCTOR

December and January were banner months for the doctors. That was when the Hong Kong flu was the "in" thing and all the doctors who had the new serum were strong-arming their patients to have shots.

It is not generally known how this flu germ got its name. I am able to divulge now, from a highly fallible source, that early in December a group of medicine men called in the creative genius of a Madison Avenue advertising agency to initiate a campaign that would combat the slump in doctors' offices due to the Christmas shopping rush.

He suggested that the Asian flu of the past was now out. "That's last year's Kleenex," he said. "We have to come up with a new name. Something scary and mysteriously Oriental."

One doctor arose and said, "How about the Red China flu?"

There were cries of "hear, hear."

The advertising man shook his head. "No good," he said. "We just want to scare them—not bring on WW III."

There were other suggestions. African flu was voted down because of the minority problem. An internist, who had majored in first aid to rebels in riots at medical school, suggested that the epidemic be called the George Wallace Flu. "Because when you get it," he explained, "you feel as if you've been run over by a car." The Southern block filibustered that suggestion.

Hong Kong flu was the final compromise. And the advertising man said, "Now look, you gotta play it cool. Let 'em get the idea that this Hong Kong serum is in short supply. Make it hard to get; that's when consumers want it most."

And so for two months the doctors reaped the harvest that their needles sewed. A patient would come to have a speck removed from his eye and the doctor would suggest a Hong Kong flu shot.

"This is hard to get, you know," he would say.

The patient would forget about his smarting eye as he walked out holding tightly to his arm, practically a basket case.

I, too, was one of the lucky patients. My doctor had the serum, which he told me he was shooting into his favorite patients. He shot it into me. It worked perfectly. The next morning, I had it.

I phoned him at home before he left for his office. I used my standard delicate approach. "Doc," I said, "you know that Hong Kong flu shot you gave me yesterday? Well, I got it."

"That's ridiculous," he said.

"Well I have a temperature. I just took it; it's 102."

"Was that orally?" he asked.

"Why? Do you want it in writing?"

He hung up. But I knew what I had to do. Lie in bed, drink plenty of fluids, and take aspirin. For ten days I lay there. I ached. My hands shook. My teeth rattled. I couldn't read. But in more desperate moments I could watch daytime television.

Do you know what it is to lie there with the Hong Kong flu, *and* with a Hong Kong flu shot in your arm, and watch *Girl Talk,* and *Snap Judgment,* and *Hollywood Squares,* and reruns of *Make Room for Daddy?* Along with all their attendant commercials?

My recovery was sudden and miraculous. It came when I learned my flu-shooting doctor had been bedded for a week with the thing. It was not that he had forgotten to give himself a shot. He just can't stand the pain of his needle.

Anyway, by mid-February the epidemic had run its course. The patients were back to 98.6, a temperature at which no physician can operate successfully.

As a result, the Madison Avenue man was called in again. His suggestion was a stroke of genius: "A March Clearance Sale of Hong Kong flu shots. No more than two to a customer."

15. MAN OF MEDICINE

I was invited recently to lecture in Philadelphia to the School of Pharmacy of Temple University, one of the finest and most advanced institutions for teaching the art of compounding and dispensing prescriptions.

You may think there is some incongruity in my appearance at a pharmacy school, but during the twenty years of my hypochondria, my bathroom cabinet became world-renowned as Junior Walgreen. Visiting doctors (in the old days when they used to visit) were astounded to discover in it every medicine from A to Z. From Achromycin to Zactirin, and, backwards, from Zyloprim to Amphojel.

Not being a legally registered pharmacist, I don't compound or dispense the stuff. I take it. It is an accepted fact in Manhattan that I, singlehandedly, kept more pharmacies going from 1940 to 1960 than "O. J., and English muffins lightly buttered, and draw one regular."

During those years, whenever I walked into a drugstore and handed the pharmacist a new prescription, I had the feeling he saw me as through an X-ray. Familiar with every detail of my anatomy, he could call off the number of my red and white corpuscles to the penny, knew to the dot how many specks I saw before my eyes.

We were on a first-name basis. I called the pharmacists "Doc," diminutive for Doctor, and they called me "Hypo," diminutive for "Here he comes again." The prescriptions they filled didn't help me, hypochondria being described by old Doc Webster in his *Unabridged* as a state of mind that dwells on imaginary ailments. But I did manage to break the complex and highly classified price code the Docs scribble on their bottles and boxes of patented medicines. And what I could tell you about that!

Given that background, you can now understand the awe and reverence in which I am held by the students of Temple's School of Pharmacy, which, incidentally, also houses the university's School of Dentistry. Many dentists were in the audience, and it was a pleasant diversion to talk to a dentist without a bale of cotton stuffed under my upper lip.

The fame of my intake of a multitude of medicines had preceded me; so these neophyte manipulators of the mortar and pestle listened with rapt attention to my talk, marveling at my ability to stand upright before them for one solid hour. Encouraged by several bursts of applause that interrupted the lecture, especially after every off-color story (don't be so surprised—druggists have their moments, too), I went on to offer several reforms for the druggists.

It was high time, I suggested, that the old custom of stuffing cotton into the top of a bottle of pills or capsules be eliminated. During my years of research, I had asked many druggists why the cotton. Only one had an answer, which I don't accept.

"The cotton," he said, "is for stuffing in your ears so you won't hear yourself screaming from the pain."

Another reform I suggested was a speed-up in filling a prescription. Nowadays you go to a druggist, who takes about one minute to count out a dozen pills and put them into a bottle, while you stand there in a cold sweat in the last stages of pneumonia, and the druggist takes ten or fifteen minutes to type out the label on the bottle. I realize how difficult it is to get a bottle into a typewriter, but shouldn't there be a course in pharmacy schools that includes speed-typing?

A third and sorely needed reform should be made in another, but kindred, department of a pharmacy. There is too much celery in the tuna fish salad. Celery is anathema to a diverticulum. Each time I complained about it, a druggist sold me a bottle of Pepto-Bismol.

And finally, but most important, is the disappearance of the friendly neighborhood pharmacist, who once upon a time could be depended on for on-the-spot treatment of a man in pain. I recall when you could walk into a drugstore and ask Doc to remove a speck from your eye. With quick, deft, surgical hands, he removed it.

Not anymore. Now, according to the new Hippocratic oath, he suggests you see a specialist. The last such specialist I was sent to operated under the high-priced degree of "ophthalmologist." He removed the speck, examined both eyes, and mumbled something about a seeing-eye dog.

Getting a druggist these days to give you that old personal attention is like pulling teeth. That, no doubt, is why Temple University has the pharmacists and dentists in the same building.

Flotsam

All I Don't Know Is
What I Read in the Papers

16. BREATHES THERE A MAN

Twenty-two years ago, on July 1, 1946, the United States moved the inhabitants of Bikini Atoll to another atoll in the Marshall Islands so that our government could conduct some underwater atomic bomb tests.

Now President Johnson has announced that the Bikini Atoll is safe again, and that the natives could return to their homes. So a committee of nine Bikini islanders came back to Bikini to investigate and to report to their countrymen on the state of the tiny island which has been kept clear of human inhabitants since 1946.

"The island is changed," *The New York Times* reported the high commissioner to have said. "Most of the trees have gone."

This remark must not have set too well with our government man in charge of making this move back to Bikini.

"Look," he said, "you people have been hollering you want to come back home. Remember, home is where you hang your hat."

"I know," replied the dissident Bikini islander. "But all the hall trees have been blown away, too. The island is not the same."

"That's what you said when we moved you away from here twenty-two years ago to Rongerik Atoll. So we moved you to the Kili Atoll. Now when you say you want to come back to Bikini, you're complaining about this atoll. If you keep raising issues like that, how can you have a life of law and order on this atoll? Seems to me you people don't like any atoll at all."

"Well," said the Bikinian, "when you moved us to Rongerik Atoll, we found poisonous fish in the lagoon."

"So we moved you to Kili Island. Besides, all our scientists have stated quite clearly that radiation levels have dropped to a point where Bikini is safe again for habitation."

"Yes, I know they said that. But I don't see any of them habitating up here. There must still be some radiation."

"Oh, I suppose there will always be a little bit of radiation. But it's safe for you to live with."

"Well, maybe for me, yes. But some of our women are a little bit pregnant. They want to be sure that their newborn . . ."

"There you go raising issues again. Let's take it from the top. You will agree that our country had to make these underwater atomic tests, right?"

"Well, we don't understand why they . . ."

"Why? Because our country is trying to get a nonproliferation treaty signed. We want all nations to sign it. How could the United States sign a nonproliferation treaty if we didn't test enough atomic bombs so we could get some proliferation to nonproliferate with?"

"How's that again?"

"You people refuse to understand."

"What we don't understand is why you picked our homeland to shoot off so many atomic bombs?"

"Why? To contain Communism. Don't you know if one small country falls, the next one topples and then they all topple. That's the domino theory."

"Yes, but we think of it as the chess theory. It seems to us we're the pawns, and we've been rooked by the kings and queens."

"Nobody's doing anything to you. Our government is going to rehabilitate this whole island. That concrete blockhouse over there is coming down; also that giant communication tower in the jungle back there. On this beach here is going to rise the new, magnificent Hilton Bikini. Do you think we'd build a big hotel if it weren't safe? Didn't you hear General Curtis LeMay say that since those atomic tests were exploded here even the rats on Bikini have grown bigger and fatter? Now don't quote me saying the Hilton Bikini is going to have fat rats. I didn't say that."

"But we don't need a hotel. We need hospitals and . . ."

"OK, we'll build you a hospital."

"Then there are all our little children."

"OK, we'll build them a schoolhouse."

"Our culture is a mixture of Polynesian and Melanesian blood."

"Oh, I get you. So we'll build two schools. We'll even give you the buses to bus the kids. What do you say, you going to move back here?"

"Well, we're just a committee of nine. We must report to our people in Kili."

"OK, you do that. Tell 'em we're going to make this an island of paradise. We'll build playgrounds, a Disneyland. We'll give you houses, Coca-Cola, churches, roads. In no time at all you'll be getting social security, welfare, unemployment insurance. Tell 'em an atom bomb that gives you all this can't be all that bad."

17. LOW FINANCE

In these times of rising prices, I have become a comparison shopper. I compare the price of a shirt with my bank balance, and wind up turning the cuffs of my old shirt.

All prices have been creeping upward. Like my shorts. So when the price of a new shirt went higher than the size of my collar, I became a comparison shopper. And it didn't comfort me when the salesman, to justify the rise, said, "Even the cost of this tag on which the price is printed has gone up."

Also my dentist. As he was pecking away at the root of a tooth that seemed to be imbedded in my tonsil, he remarked that the cord on his grinding machine used to cost 20 cents. Now it is $8. This extra bite showed up on his bill the following month.

What could I do? You just can't gad about comparison-shopping strange dentists who are not familiar with every bi- and tricuspid in your mouth, can you?

Otherwise, comparison shopping has made me a wiser

buyer. In a doughnut shop where once I enjoyed a glazed doughnut and a cup of coffee for a quarter, the price is now 45 cents. Luckily, I was able to solve this exorbitant rise with a visit to my doctor at which we decided glazed doughnuts were not good for me, I told him.

But one place where comparison shopping doesn't help is the stock market. I'm not too familiar with the inner workings of this august money-making institution, but I've discovered it's a monopoly. In my comparison shopping, I've found all brokerage houses have conspired to show the same prices for all stocks. I stayed away.

Until the day I got this hot tip from an unimpeachable source. It was our President, saying to a group of businessmen, "If I had the money, I'd buy stocks now."

Well, I didn't have the money either, but I do have this home I own in Key Biscayne, Florida, and another in San Clemente, California. I mortgaged them.

I was at the broker's office a half-hour before the market opened. Waiting for the bell, I felt sorry our President didn't have the money to take advantage of his own hot tip. I vowed that by my being scrupulously honest to the penny and by even adding a few dollars to help balance his budget, I would show my appreciation to Mr. Nixon for all this money I was going to make.

I scanned the board for some good stocks to buy. It didn't really matter. They're all good. Didn't he say, "Buy stocks now"? But to be certain of the investment, I decided to buy only blue chip stocks. Whatever they are. Actually, they were all blue chips. "Buy stocks now." I'll buy some cheap blue chips in the ten- or twelve-dollar range. I don't want to set the world on fire, just start a small flame under my bank account.

The bell! I sprang into action. Buy twenty-five shares of this. Buy twenty-five of that. Twenty-five of these, those, and them! I wanted to beat the other customers to the bargain prices. But as I looked around, nobody had sprung into action but me. I deduced they hadn't read the morning paper. I left there loaded with stocks.

On my way home, I passed the doughnut shop. I went in. Glazed doughnuts, I decided, weren't all that bad for me. I had two. In another few hours I would be well on the road to Fort Knox.

Well, what can I tell you? When that day ended, I was well on the road to San Luis Rey. The days and weeks that followed were nightmarish. How had I been so foolish, I kept asking myself. How had I forgotten I was a comparison shopper? How had he known I hadn't voted for him?

Then suddenly one morning somebody in Washington turned on the hot money faucet. Stocks went up thirty points the first day, twenty points up the second day. There was dancing in the streets of Wall, there were laughter and lighthearted banter.

But not for me. One of my stocks went up an eighth of a point, another went down a fourth of a point, and two dropped off of the Big Board down to the Over-the-Counter market. My own private crash.

Now, *nouveau pauvre*, I went to my banker for a loan to cover the margin. He said they don't lend money to play the stock market. I said I'll lose my shirt. He said that's no big loss. He must have noticed the turned cuffs.

18. YOU SAY TOMENTOSE;
I SAY TOMAHNTOSE

In one of his recent speeches Vice President Agnew referred to our rebellious youths as "those tomentose exhibitionists." That sent me running to my unabridged:

"tomentose, adj. (L. *tomentum*) . . . Covered with densely matted hairs."

OK. Let's take it from there:

On the evening of July 3, 1776, a group of tomentose revolutionaries had finished writing and rewriting a declaration that signified their desire for independence from the Establishment.

Tempestuous young Tom Jefferson, the author of the paper, his tomentum curled in a bob over his coat collar, held those truths to be so self-evident that he was for everybody's signing it then and there.

But wise old Ben Franklin shook his tomentous mane and said, according to the old joke, "Not yet. Let's wait until tomorrow, the Fourth of July, so this event may always be celebrated on a national holiday."

This met with the approval of the other rebels, tomentose and tomentulose alike, and the parchment was signed on July 4. After which they all posed for a group painting, a photographed copy of which I have here. And what a tomentose sight it is!

That of course led to the signing of another paper eleven years later. This one was written by a whole Congress of tomenta, and it began: "We, the people of the United States, in order to form a more perfect Union . . ."

Just how much "more" than "perfect" anything can be has over the years been my hang-up. But I always figured it was the overwrought exuberance of some young dissident with a tomentose problem.

I have often wondered why it wasn't modified to "a *more nearly* perfect Union" by some discerning member of that Continental Congress. No matter if he was glabrous or barbigerous. (Our Vice President knows what I mean.)

The Declaration of Independence and the Constitution were signed after weeks of stormy debates. Yet, history does not record that even one of the signers saw fit to heckle opponents by referring to anyone's hairstyle or his mode of dress.

That's the gap in the style of debate between the 1770s and the 1970s. Today, the issues are diverted, and the dissenters are called effete, snobbish, tomentose bums. This is not to say that the tomentose group has not also indulged itself in unattractive namecalling—"Pigs," "Fascists," "Nazis." And the childish "They started it" is not a substantive argument.

That kind of last resort, name-calling debate is a page borrowed from the joke books of nightclub comedians.

When a comic is heckled by a patron who has drunk up
his entire cover charge and is in the mellow mood for
free and open debate on any subject, the comedian is
well prepared for him.

Hoping to quiet the inebriate, the comic goes into his
sure-fire "personal insult" routines. Any nightclub ha-
bitué will recall these so-called Milton Berleish ad libs:

"Yes, sir, you wear that suit, don't you care what anybody says?" he says to the unruly patron. Or "Did you
take your ugly pill today?" Or "I remember you, madame,
you heckled me ten years ago in Pittsburgh. I never forget a dress." Or "Will you please move over, sir, your
head is shining in my eyes."

One-liners about a dissident student's hair or style of
dress only diffuse the issues that divide us. What does it
profit a man, especially one in high office, to castigate
the cut of a student's jacket or the length of his tomentum
or the open toes of his sandals?

The "insult" routines are not confined only to men in
high office. The funny part is that many aging male private citizens who deride the tomentose students are ap-
ing them, hair for hair, dress for dress. All window
dressing—mostly bay window.

It is not uncommon to hear a man put down long-
haired students, while he himself sports graying side-
burns down to his mandible, jacket lapeled to his ears,
and trousers so tight as to cut off what little circulation
he still has.

These old gentlemen use the young's rhetoric. They
call the long-haired kids "uptight." The young folks make
them "blow their minds." They sound "groovy," but it's

only their dress and hair that are young. Their thinking is old.

Our great nation polarized and divided against itself. Where is that promised "coming together"? One can only hope that some year soon a Fourth of July will be celebrated as "Interdependence Day."

19. THE SORE LOSER

When the last election was a few days off, the tension at our house had grown perceptibly; chaos could not be far behind. For weeks, she had sat before the TV set making copious notes on every appearance of the two-and-a-half candidates running for the Presidency and on the issues for which they campaigned.

After years of apathy, she was this time trying to sort out her choice for President. She had become so deeply involved that I found myself with a New Politics rebel on my hands. And aside from hitting her over the head with a nightstick, I didn't know how to handle it.

Until that election her voting had been an uncomplicated happening—a trip to the beauty parlor and then to the polling booth. ("You have to look your nicest when you're voting for President. I don't want to go in there looking like the wrath of grapes.") And she always has managed to vote early. ("I want to get there before Huntley and Brinkley tell me how I voted.")

She picked that night as I was falling asleep to offer

me the privilege, for the first time, to see the notes she
had been taking.

"I can't sleep," she said. "I've been lying here tossing—
first heads, then tails. I'm worried about this election.
And it's your fault mostly. Didn't you promise me the
No. 1 issue was going to be how to stop the war in Vietnam?"

"Well, I didn't exactly promise it."

"But the candidates didn't say how. Look at these
notes. Put on your glasses."

"Don't you think it's too late for that now?"

"To put on your glasses? You know you can't see without them no matter what time it is. Look at these notes."

"What does this mean—f-a-n-t-o-m?"

"Oh, that was the other day—Nixon said he would send
Israel phantom jets."

"That's P-h-a-n-t-o-m as in *Phantom of the Opera*."

"Dear, this is no time for grammar. We're picking a President."

"Are you opposed to sending Phantom jets?"

"Of course not. And while they're at it, why not send
phantom soldiers and phantom bullets?"

"Uh—yes. Now, what does this mean—this can't be
streetwalkers, can it?"

"Sure, that's what it is. That's George Wallace."

"What's George Wallace?"

"Didn't he say he wants to make the streets safe for
streetwalkers?"

"You do mean, I hope, that he wants to make sure
everyone can walk safely in the streets without being
shot at?"

"That's it. That's because it's so easy to get guns nowadays."

"Yes, they're very popular. That's why we need new gun laws. There are too many guns being freely passed out into the hands of our young citizens."

"Yes, especially by our army."

"Can I quote you on that?"

"Of course you can believe it. No candidate wants to talk much about ending the war. That's what makes it so hard to decide whom to vote for. Do you have any idea how much the war costs every day?"

"About $100 million a day."

"Yes. And that's a lot of aughts. If we took that money and spent it on the poor people, we could build up the slums and the ghettos and those old testament houses."

"Holy Moses."

"Well, doesn't it to you?"

"Yes, I think it does. What does this mean in your notes here—'Sunny . . . HHH.'"

"Oh, that was the weather man. He said it was going to rain, and it turned out to be a beautiful, sunny day."

"What's Hubert Horatio Humphrey got to do with that?"

"Oh, that's not Humphrey—that's HHH, ha ha ha. I was laughing at the weather man."

"Of course, how stupid of me. Well, maybe that's a good omen. It could indicate that if you vote for Humphrey, everything will be sunny from here on out."

"How about that? Yes, maybe that's a good omen. He is very jolly. Of course. That's it. Thank you, dear."

"Oh, it was nothing. May I go to sleep now?"

"Of course, dear. Thanks for helping me. Everything

got so complicated. Why can't they simplicate it like it always was? They don't make elections like they used to, do they, dear?"

"No, I guess they . . ."

"When you listen to all these candidates on television on all those panel shows, it's a regular baffle of wits who to vote for. But after talking it over with you I feel better about it. Thank you again, dear."

"You're more than welcome. Goodnight, Jane."

"Goodnight, Chet."

I will now demonstrate how dangerous a little knowledge can be. As we sat before our set on election night, she said, "I'll bet you Humphrey wins the election."

It was like stealing. She has plenty of money. Years ago, she invested heavily in 2-cent stamps. And you know what it costs to send a letter today. "I've tripled my money," she said.

I tried to dissuade her. "Save your money," I said. "You'll only lose. Nixon is a shoo-in. All the polls have told us that."

"Well, at least I'm glad you didn't say Pollacks, like you-know-who. Those polls don't fool me. All those campaign speeches Nixon made with the balloons flying, and the spaghetti throwing. I'll still bet you Humphrey wins."

So we made a bet. And now we're having a drink before dinner the evening after the election. I didn't want to bring up the unpleasant subject of some money changing hands. I led to it tactfully.

"Well," I said, "it was very close, but you sure lost that bet, didn't you?"

"I lost the election, that's the bad part. And that's what

I get for listening to you. Didn't you promise me there were millions more Democrats than Republicans?"

"Well, I didn't exactly promise."

"And didn't you tell me the people will all vote for Humphrey because they can always vote for Nixon next time?"

"That was a little joke, Jane."

"There's a time to joke, and a time not. And this was not."

"You're just mad because you lost a bet. Why don't you pay up and we'll eat. I'm hungry. What's for dinner?"

"Meatballs and confetti. And I'm not mad. I'm more uh—I'm scared."

"Scared! You're kidding."

"Oh, no? Did you notice I'm not wearing my Humphrey button any more? What are we going to do now? Where can we go?"

"Go? Hey, you're climbing walls. Cool it. This is America. We're all one big family. Every four years we have our family squabbles; then when they're over, we get together again and go forward. We all have to live in one big house with whatever President is elected. Now we have to live with Nixon."

"Well, I'll live with him, but I won't have any children."

"What on earth does that mean?"

"So they can send them to war? Not me. Never. And if I'm wrong, I'm not far from it."

"Oh, I get it, Lysistrata, hmm?"

"Beg pardon?"

"You remember—the Peloponnesian War—lasted twenty years. Lysistrata resented seeing the men going off to war all the time, so she decided not to live with her husband any more. She was the Greek lady."

"Please, dear, that's not nice. Don't bring her into it. She just got married."

"Oh, sorry. Of course. But you're all wrong about Nixon. He's for ending the war. Didn't you hear him saying he has a solution to end the war, and as soon as he becomes President January 20, he's going to tell us how?"

"That's what I didn't understand. It's like a doctor who says he's found a cure for cancer but he won't tell us what it is till January 20."

"January 20—is that the day you're going to pay me the bet you lost?"

"The one I really feel sorry for is Senator McCarthy."

"I didn't bet him."

"What happened to all those young people who were for McCarthy? Why didn't they vote for Humphrey?"

"Most of them were not of voting age."

"That's it. Aren't you in favor of lowering the voting age?"

"At which end?"

"Beg pardon?"

"I think the voting age should definitely be lowered. Nobody over sixty should be allowed to vote. They're all lobbying for Social Security, old age pensions, and Medicare. Now pay up and let's forget the election. OK?"

"Forget it? I won't forget this election if I live to be as old as Macushla. How can I forget Senator McCarthy? What's going to become of him with all those Republicans all over the place?"

"I think that's unfair. You can't hold the Republicans responsible for the shape the world's in today."

"Well, who do you think is responsible for the shape the world's in today?"

"Rand McNally."

"Oh, him. Well, I'm glad he didn't get in with that George Wallace."

"That was LeMay."

"Whatever."

"Why don't you just pay me the money you lost and let's—"

"Oh, all right. Here's your money."

"Well don't throw it at me."

"I didn't throw it. You let it fall on purpose. Now pick up your quarter and let's eat."

20. DO WRITE AND FEAR NO MAN

There was a time when Western Union used to advertise, "Don't Write, Telegraph." That's changed. Take the story in *The New York Times* concerning a man who telephoned a telegram to WU, addressed to President Nixon after the expansion of the war into Cambodia.

"Your bum lies—"

That's as far as he got when, according to the newspaper, the Western Union operator cut in: "I am sorry, Sir, you can't say that. If you have constructive criticism to offer, OK. But why not send a letter instead?"

The man persisted, so the operator took it up with her supervisor who finally OK'd the telegram, which read: YOUR BUM LIES ABOUT CAMBODIA MURDERED KENT FOUR. END WAR NOW.

A friend of this man, the paper says, sent another telegram: YOUR PERVERTED AND OBSCENE LYING WILL LEAD US ALL TO SLAUGHTER. END WAR NOW. This was accepted with no demurral.

Without going into the editorial policy of Western

Union, one can surmise there are hawks and doves among the operators who will let you know where they stand the minute you start dictating a telegram. They telegraph their punches.

I like better what the first operator said, "Why not send a letter instead?" But why not a telegram *and* a letter? How would that go? First I telephone my wire, but there is a communication gap—the operator objecting to one word in the message.

To please her, I alter the telegram to read: DEAR MR. PRESIDENT: I ADORE THE WAY YOU HAVE EXPANDED THE WAR INTO CAMBODIA. I argue that this slightly alters the message I am conveying, and she suggests I write a letter. I say I will.

But first I send a wire: DEAR MR. PRESIDENT: IGNORE FIRST TELEGRAM, LETTER FOLLOWS. Then I write the letter:

"Dear Mr. President: By now you must have read both my telegrams, and are anxiously awaiting an explanation. What it was was, I had this thing with this Western Union operator, who is apparently an extreme and violent fan of your war.

"She objected to the second word in my message, which in the original version was not 'adore,' but 'I abhor the way you have expanded the war into Cambodia.' She objected to the word 'abhor'—well, not exactly the whole word, it was more the second syllable.

"Mr. President, I tried to make the meaning crystal clear to her, in a nonviolent way, of course, because you have always said you favor dissent if it's nonviolent. You will be pleased to know that my voice was lowered to a point where I was speechless.

"As her dialogue became more and more heated, she

told me that instead of sending telegrams, I should get my hair cut, and stop burning down buildings on my campus, and even suggested that I was an aquaphobe.

"By this time I was pretty nervous. The thought came to me that maybe I was in violation of some obscure Morse Code of Morals, and would be subject to arrest by Western Union, or to some other wrath which God hath wrought.

"Outwardly, however, I kept my cool. And when the operator had simmered down to tepid, I apologized. I said it was my mistake. I hadn't meant to write 'abhor,' it should have been 'adore.'

"Anyway, in spite of my dissent, please be informed that my prayers are with you in your devout resolution to abort the killings. I would have sent that in a telegram, but I'm sure one word there would start her off again.

"And now, Mr. President, a little humor to lighten the awesome burden of your office. Censoring telegrams is not new. Thirty years ago, Noël Coward was in a play in New York. He received a letter from a friend in England saying he was coming to New York. Mr. Coward went to the telegraph office in his hotel and wrote a telegram: 'Looking forward to your arrival, will give you keys to the city.' He signed it 'Mayor LaGuardia.'

"The operator said, 'You are not allowed to use the name of a famous person to sign a telegram.'

"Mr. Coward tore it up and composed another: 'Looking forward to your arrival, will give you keys to the city.' He signed it 'Noël Coward.'

"The operator was furious. 'I said you can't sign the name of a famous person.'

"'But, Madame,' said Mr. Coward, 'I *am* Noël Coward.'"

"'Oh, really?' she said. 'Well, in that case you can sign it 'Mayor LaGuardia.'"

"Well, Mr. President, I hope you got a chuckle out of that. I am respectfully yours, in peace, Spiro. (Ha, ha.)"

21. TWO THOUGHTS OF SCHOOL

Recently in New York's City University there occurred the most polite campus revolt on record. Fifteen students of the John Jay College of Criminal Justice quietly walked out of class and resigned from the school, because they didn't agree with something the professor had said.

The fifteen students were agents of the Federal Bureau of Investigation, taking a course in criminal justice. What the professor had said was critical of the head of the FBI. The fifteen students agreed the professor had the right to say it, but they claimed they didn't have to sit there and listen to it.

So, without burning a building, or locking up a dean, or closing a school, they staged this exemplary, non-violent campus rebellion. It was Page 1 in *The New York Times*. But it is to the shame of television that not a single camera was there to record fifteen students softly tiptoeing out of a classroom in high dudgeon.

What an opportunity it could have been for the TV networks to demonstrate, for the kids watching the news-

casts, the difference between anarchy and peaceful revolt. Months earlier they had cameras all over Kent State
when the National Guard had been called in to quell a
students' uprising.

That bit of campus unrest resulted in a grand jury's
absolving the National Guard of blame and arresting
twenty-five students, non-students, and members of the
faculty. The charge against them was apparently loiter-
ing in front of a moving bullet.

I have been a fan of non-violence since my days in
grammar school. This was because I was reared in a
broken home. That is, my mother's attitude toward me
was peaceably permissive; my father's was negatively de-
cisive. A home can't be more broken than that (violins
only here, softly).

From the age of nine, it was I who was the object of
their divisiveness. When I told them I wanted, or thought
I needed, all the things any boy of nine or ten thinks he
wants or needs, a great debate took place. As it grew
more heated, I was always sent to my room. But I could
always hear, and still can, the softly permissive voice of
my mother, and the fiery negative decision by my father.

When I came down to breakfast the next morning I
was not surprised that my mother had won—she won most
of the time. But what did surprise me was the loving attitude displayed by my parents for each other, after the
violent confrontation of the night before. How they managed to live in blissful compatibility all through my form-
ative years was beyond my youthful ken.

The most hectic debate took place the day I came
home from school with a note from my fourth-grade

teacher saying I had to be fitted for a pair of glasses. My father reacted as though I had just spindled his computer card.

"Glasses for a boy ten years old?" he shouted. "He's got plenty of time for glasses when he's forty. If he didn't spend so much time looking at stereopticon slides, he wouldn't need glasses. Two weeks of no stereopticon," he said to me.

"Go to your room, dear," my mother said.

I went. But the following morning my mother went with me to get the glasses. Another victory for non-violence, but that's how it rubbed off on, and stayed with, me to this day.

However, I should confess the complete story of the glasses. There was nothing wrong with my eyes. It was my id that was at fault. I had developed a crush on my fourth-grade teacher, but because I sat in the last row, she seldom called on me to give an answer, or ever noticed me.

I asked if I could exchange seats with a boy in the first row, and she refused. I told her I couldn't see the blackboard. She wrote the note. While the glasses were being made, she let me temporarily change seats with a boy who never knew the answers and was glad to sit in the back row. Chalk up another triumph for a non-violently attained goal.

But horror of horrors! Hoisted by my own petard! This teacher who, from the back row, seemed a beautiful woman of twenty, now that I was up closer, turned out to be an old woman of forty. A Pyrrhic victory!

Actually, the glasses were a tricky and dishonest goal. While no one denies the rights of students to protest against an obvious and flagrant injustice, there are, however, some far-out goals that, after being fought for, could turn out to be a "woman of forty" when young students get seats up closer to life.

22. MARTHA OF WASHINGTON

When a man walks into an elevator and says to the operator, "Thirty-eight East Fifty-seventh Street," one of two things is happening to him: Something is preying on his mind, or he's lost his other marble.

Contrary to what you may deduce, something has been preying on my mind. It's our freedom to speak out. We're losing it. Not only you and I, but some big people connected with the Nixon administration are being quietly shushed. For instance, the attractive and colorfully eloquent Martha Mitchell, wife of John N., Attorney General.

Just because she telephoned a newspaper at 3 in the morning demanding the editor "crucify" Senator Fulbright, it was suggested by some nervous bureaucrat that it would be prudent to get Martha a Press Secretary to calm her stream of conscious rhetoric so it wouldn't make that many waves.

That incident started a trend because, after Mr. Mitchell had embarrassed our President with the names of two judges not acceptable to the Senate, and he issued a statement that agitated the polluted political waters of the Potomac, Mr. Mitchell got a Press Secretary.

Two Press Secretaries—His and Hers—a man for Mr. Mitchell, a woman for Martha. It might have been more exciting the other way, but that's a different column. The point is, when freedom of speech of any two persons is aborted, all citizens lose a little freedom. Not to mention the loss of some spicy, internecine Washington gossip.

Press Secretary is upper-case jargon for press agent. A press agent is an image maker. To repair images of public officials so that their uninspired statements seem like what they're not demands a skilled press agent who can defend his client against the slanted headlines in the biased press.

When the client finds himself on the horns of a dilemma, the press agent's duty is to grab the bull by the tail, so that when the bull looks around to see what's holding him up, the client slips quickly off the horns, rushes home to take a shower, and dashes to his office to meet the reporters.

"I beg your pardon," he asks innocently. "What bull are you talking about? I don't know anything about a bull."

It works like this: "Here's what I'll do, Mr. Mitchell," says the press agent. "After you slip off the horns of your dilemma, I'll let go of the tail, and write a speech putting the blame on the Senate for turning down your two judges because they were Southerners. And, instead of your making the speech, I'll give it to the Vice President to deliver somewhere. Preferably in a town down South."

Vice President Agnew is Press Secretary without portfolio, in full control of his freedom to speak out. The V.P. went to Columbia, South Carolina, where he castigated the Senate for its antipathy to Southerners. He was a big hit. Encouraged by the applause, Mr. Agnew added still another jewel to the crown of the Attorney General. He pointed out there had been a dramatic drop in the rise of crime in the streets since Mr. Mitchell took office. The rate had dropped from 29 per cent when Ramsey Clark was Attorney General to only 13 per cent under Mr. Mitchell.

"The crime rate," Mr. Agnew was quoted, "is being brought under control by strong executive action in the Justice Department."

This extravagant credit given to Martha's husband is pure Barnum and Bailey. You and I know where the real credit belongs: To our citizens who have barricaded themselves in their homes, afraid to venture out at night. You simply can't have as many muggers on the streets to commit crimes, if there aren't as many muggees for the muggers to mug. Right?

Even the President has a Press Secretary. But when Mr. Nixon wants to reach out to the people for support, he orders a half-hour of television time. Mr. Nixon's career on TV has been checkered. Remember? But now, as befits a man in the highest office, TV is his "room," as the actors put it.

So masterfully does he convey an intimate closeup of a man alone, on the horns of a dilemma, with no press agent to diminish his anguish—a Commander-in-Chief so dedicated to bringing home his armed forces that he must expand the war into Cambodia—that 80 per cent of his telephone calls applauded the expansion.

Sad. We are caught on the horns of a technocracy where our government can bring three men back alive from 250,000 miles around the moon, but we can't bring 250,000 men back alive from 8,000 miles across the Pacific.

23. PEACE AND WAR

You don't need a crystal ball to foresee how crystal-clear it is that the peace talks in Paris will continue to move at an *escargot's* pace. If indeed they will ever get going at all.

My private State Department, which I am Secretary of, has two simple solutions. If they are acted on in combination, they will bring about a quick, just, honorable, face-saving peace before the next happy announcement that *only* eighty-eight American boys were killed in the past week. The plan:

1) North Vietnam should take immediate steps to Vietnamize the peace talks by sending back their chief negotiator, who left the peace table and went back to Hanoi.

Of course, Vietnamization is not an overnight, instant-coffee thing. It would entail our State Department's sending advisers and technicians to train the Hanoi negotiator in the art of diplomacy, patience, etiquette.

2) Move the peace talks out of Paris at once. It is obvious the North Vietnamese still in the City of Light are

having a love affair with La Belle France. That's something you don't hurry to get back to your wife in Hanoi.

The North Vietnamese love Paris in the springtime; they love it in the summer. They love Paris when it drizzles; they love it when it sizzles. No monsoons in Paris. As far as they're concerned, the peace talks can go on for many, many seasons to come. They can go on till Defense Secretary Melvin Laird freezes over.

Paris is something you don't forget too easily. Paris uncovers a multitude of sins that a peace delegate can readily turn into a *joie de vivre*. I'll bet if the peace talks were moved to Provo, Utah, peace would be declared in an hour.

It's not that the North Vietnamese in Paris are not mixing a little business in with their Parisian pleasures. Just enough to justify their expense accounts.

I have here a page out of a day's diary carefully kept by one Phan Brand Nu. Judging by some of the items he hopes to get away with, you can tell how brand new he is at the expense account game. I quote:

"Spent morning sending post cards of the Louvre, Eiffel Tower, Arc de Triomphe, and the Champs Elysées. Many friends have written me to keep those French post cards coming." (I told you he was new at the game.)

"Made my daily trip to Napoleon's Tomb." (Even a visit to Napoleon lying in state is heaven to what's waiting for him in Hanoi.)

"At 5 o'clock in the evening with Phan Wats Nu, and with Phan Hey Nonny Nu, for cocktails at Harry's Bar. Wats and I had two martinis. Hey Nonny was induced by the bartender to try a new drink called a Mickey.

"Later, Wats and I went to dinner." (Obviously Hey Nonny threw up his hands, and everything, and called it a night.)

"We had dinner again at Maxim's. Used my credit card." (The North Vietnam Master Charge.)

"After dinner Wats and I strolled over to the Tuileries for our nightly mission to convert Parisians to our cause. In the dark we spied two likely prospects standing at one of the fountains. We spoke to them at some length, and they appeared quite willing to collaborate. The blonde one particularly was warmly receptive. They promised they would meet us at this spot tomorrow night. Then, as is the custom with all loyal revolutionaries, they disappeared abruptly into the darkness." (Oh boy! There's something peculiar going on here.)

"After that we went directly to the Folies-Bergère, which we have infiltrated since coming to Paris. But as I went to pay for our tickets, I was astounded to discover I had no money. It must have dropped out en route from the gardens." (See? What did I tell you?)

"I asked Wats for money, and he too had dropped his en route." (Rolled! And these are the guys it's taking us so long to lick?)

"We hurried back to our hotel to get money from Hey Nonny. He was in bed, and, though we shook him to make him understand our plight, he stared at us uncomprehendingly." (Vive la Mickey!)

"We finally gave up and borrowed the money from his pants pocket." (Good thinking.)

"Then we hurried back to wind up our work at the Folies-Bergère."

Some work! That's what I've been trying to tell you—
move the peace talks to Provo, Utah. As long as they're
in Paris they'll be winding up at the Folies-Bergère,
instead of winding up the Folies de Guerre.

24. TO DREAM THE IMPLAUSIBLE DREAM

I am an early riser—6:30 a.m. It's not that I have a nightly problem drifting off to dreamland. It's simply that at this early hour I run out of sleep.

I arise, make some notes of the dreams I've had through the tortuous night, step gingerly into the world, and hope that I may avoid their fulfillment.

So I listened with interest to our President one day last June as he addressed the Jaycee Convention in St. Louis. He said he was going to speak about "what is right about America."

"I believe in the American Dream," he stated. "I have seen it come true in my own life. But, speaking in broader terms, we can fulfill the American Dream only when every American has an equal opportunity to fulfill his own dream."

The American Dream! That's where I had gone wrong. My dreams have been un-American. Scratch that—I mean non-American. I consider myself as American as the next slice of apple pie. But my nightmarish dreams have not been national, only personal little hangups, and terrifying.

I never dreamed I dwelled in marble halls with vassals and serfs at my side. Whenever I dreamed I was in a marble hall, I was always a vassal, polishing the marble.

Instead of the American Dream, my nocturnal wanderings dealt with nothing socially significant—nothing to do with "what is right about America." Like the night I dreamed about the number seven. At the race track the next day I bet on horse number seven in the seventh race, which was 7 to 1 in the betting. And in a seven-horse race he finished seventh. That would make anyone an early riser.

But after I heard the President, I decided to tune my subliminal to another channel where, as Mr. Nixon magnanimously stated that day, "Every American has an equal opportunity to fulfill his own dreams." Where but in America does a sleeping citizen have the freedom to choose his own dreams?

As I curled myself into the arms of Morpheus that first night, I drifted off, concentrating on "what is right about America." Soon I found myself on a plane flying from Paris to London. Suddenly a hijacker appeared and ordered the plane to go to America. We landed in Augusta, Georgia, where we were met by Governor Maddox, who invited us all into his restaurant for a free chicken dinner and a slice of apple pie. It was a gala affair, except he did not allow salt and pepper shakers together on his lily-white tablecloths.

Aside from that one unpleasant bit of atavism, it was an American Dream about what is right with America. The chicken was so delicious I didn't even mind the Governor's telling us the hijacker was a Communist who wanted to come to America to integrate the schools in Georgia. Fried chicken and apple pie were a good start on what is right about America.

The next night I dreamed I dwelled in the halls of Congress, where a law was passed on rent control. "In order to stabilize the economy," a senator said, "all apartments in the nation henceforth will rent at the same price —$1,000 a month. And all bankers are authorized to lend money to apartment dwellers, employed or unemployed, so that this American Dream may be fulfilled."

I was up at 4 o'clock that morning. I couldn't wait till nightfall to dream what was going to happen at my bank. So I took a nap that afternoon and found myself facing my banker, who was unusually cheery about lending me the money. "The interest," he smiled, "will be 25 per cent."

I suggested that 25 per cent was a little high. "But wait," he said, "you haven't heard the best part. Every American has dreamed that someday he would own a toaster or an alarm clock. We offer you a freedom of choice—free—a toaster or an alarm clock." I chose the toaster. I wouldn't need an alarm clock to wake me out of that one.

After a few more nights of those dreams, I realized my dreams were not making America seem dreamy. You know why? Because all American dreamers are dreaming their own particular American Dreams, which are contradictory and antagonistic to my particular American Dreams.

But maybe dreams worked in *early* America. So I went back to my early American Dream. What was right about

America those days was Josie—the girl in high school. What is wrong about Josie these nights is that she is still quite contradictory and antagonistic to my own particular American Dream.

25. PAGING SOLOMON

For the past month, New Yorkers have disengaged themselves from the problems of inflation, unemployment, higher taxes, and related worries tugging at their purse strings. Time out was taken by all for a happening that tore at their heartstrings. And, as was to be expected in these days of accepted values not in the American mainstream, the people here are violently divided in their judgment as to whether legality was better served than morality.

Three years ago, an unwed mother, aged nineteen, signed a legal consent for the adoption of her newborn son. Fourteen months later she was in court demanding the return of her baby. The court ruled the child should be returned to its natural mother. The foster parents took the matter to the state Court of Appeals, where the lower-court ruling was recently sustained, and the three-year-old boy was handed over to his natural mother.

About a year and a half ago, this same mother had met and married another man. "I do. I do." Then she decided she could now make a home for the boy. Despite testimony by a physician and a psychiatrist that the transfer of the baby from the home and the love of his foster parents would be detrimental to this tiny human, the judge in the high court sustained the ruling that the youngster should be given to his natural mother. Court adjourned. Gavel. Finis.

The court does not ask the re-instated mother and her new husband, "Do you both promise to love and cherish this little boy, to be with him in sickness and in growing up?" There is no "I do. I do."

The judge did not offer the anguished foster mother, now near collapse, visiting rights. Nor did he suggest that she be allowed to watch the youngster, while at play, from behind a school yard fence. The law does not recognize foster love, nor the tragic void in the home of the only parents the boy had ever known.

Just reading about the final moments of the case is torment. In recounting the dialogue between the natural mother and the child, *The New York Times* reports that she said to him, "Would you like to go with me for a minute?" And the child replied, "Yes." A minute! A lifetime! He could afford a minute away from the joy of his foster parents to go with this strange woman.

So, he said, "Yes." Politely. And then the natural mother said, "Say good-by to your mommy and daddy." Mommy and daddy—so set apart from mother and father. In that one "minute," the child had acquired a mommy and a daddy, a mother and a stepfather.

"Yes," he said. Then looking up at her, the boy asked, "What is your name?" And she replied, "Betty." Mother and son on a first-name basis. Betty and Richard. Only the last name had been changed by the court to protect this little innocent.

She did not reply, "My name is Betty. I am your mother." If she had, this bright, beautiful little boy would have somehow divined that the woman meant to take him away for a minute that would last forever.

The mother led the blond little chap to the elevator, where she gathered him into her arms. And he began to struggle. "I want to go to my mommy," he said. And he reached out his little arms to the only mother he had ever known.

Justice is blind. Also deaf. However, it is not mute. When the new mother requested the court to permit her to take the boy out by a side door to avoid the newsmen, the judge denied her that privilege. "The public," he stated, according to the *Times,* "would be better served to see the terrible tragedy that can come from situations like this."

The high judge betrayed the agony that had gone into his sad decision. There was a technicality: The adoption proceedings had not been legally finalized. A foster mother's love for a child she had reared and nurtured since infancy is not a technicality recognized by any court.

The judge did not claim to have the wisdom of Solomon. His was only to follow the law to its letter. And let the hearts chip where they may.

There is nothing in the law that forbids a woman to change her mind. A woman's prerogative. I, too, am no Solomon. But it seems that foster parents, to say nothing of adopted children torn from one set of arms to another, would be better served, and tragedies avoided, if an unwed mother who gives up her baby for adoption had changed her mind earlier. As on the day she said "I will" to the man who thereupon fathered her child.

Jetsam

Old Age Is Wasted on the Elderly

26. THIRTY ON THIRTY

The Social Revolution in our nation—American pitted against American—is dangerously near to creating a society of two states, separate and unequal. Those aged thirty or under, and those over thirty.

Let it be known now and for all time that I am never again going to speak to anyone under thirty.

It's not that I haven't tried. Only this week, in the interest of vital research for this piece, I went down to Manhattan's Washington Square to interview some New York University students on their reactions to President Nixon's press conference telethon, during which he said that young rebels are against everything but they never indicate anything they are for.

Well, ending that sentence with that preposition, I went downtown and walked through the University buildings, and I came upon this young man with a guitar. I asked him if he had heard the President's statement.

"I don't listen to anybody over thirty," he said.

"But this is the President."

"What's he done so far?" he asked.

"Has it occurred to you that this is a man who has tried so hard for so long to be President that he may be finding it difficult to believe he actually made it?"

"I don't talk to anybody over thirty."

"Why, man? What's your thing? What's your hang-up?" I said trying to sound under thirty.

He stared at me, shifting his guitar from one hand and teasing his hair with the other. His apparel was rather—well, it wasn't what you could call kempt.

"I take it that being over thirty is not your bag," I said, "but just being against over-thirty is not being *for* anything."

"OK, if you want to debate," he said, "I'll tell you what I'm for. Number one, I'm against the Establishment. Number two, I think the war in Vietnam is immoral. Number three, I'm against discrimination. Number four, no old professor can dictate to me what clothes I wear. Number five, I'm against recruiting on campuses. Number six, I'm against the police not letting us demonstrate."

I don't want you to think our debate was one-sided. I got in a few "Buts" after some of those numbers. If he had stopped there, I would have walked away. But he concluded with this:

"You old people got this world in this condition. Now you have a handful of guilt, and you don't know where to put it."

He had a handful of guitar which I could have told him where to put. But I was cool.

"Hold it, man," I said. "Before we split, I'd like to lay a little something on you. What do you think would have happened to this country if nobody had ever spoken to anyone over thirty? Suppose nobody would have talked to Thomas Jefferson when he was thirty-three, when he drafted the Declaration of Independence. Or the men who signed it—Benjamin Franklin, age seventy, John Adams, forty-one, Sam Adams, fifty-four. Mathew Thornton; you haven't forgotten him, have you? He was sixty-two. Even Button Gwinnett was forty-four. To say nothing of good old Caesar Rodney, age forty-eight. And the man who put his John Hancock on it was thirty-nine. Where were you under-thirties when that piece of paper was written?

"And suppose nobody would have talked to Thomas Edison when he was forty-one and demonstrated his kinetoscope for the first time. Where would your sex movies be today?

"And how about a man who said 'I have a vaccine that will prevent polio?' Jonas Salk was forty-one. And suppose you wouldn't have listened to Robert Morse, when he said he could send a message by telegraph. He was fifty-three years old when he telegraphed 'What hath God wrought?'

"And would it surprise you to know that Wilhelm Roentgen was slightly over thirty when he came up with the X-ray machine? Fifty, to be exact. And Sir Isaac Newton established the law of gravity when he was forty-three. How do you like them apples?"

"Very interesting," he replied, "but I noticed you conveniently omitted Albert Einstein. He was only twenty-two when he wrote his theory of relativity. How does that grab you?"

"It grabs me in the pit of the stomach," I said. "If nobody had listened to that under-thirty, this world would not now be in danger of being blown out of the universe. Now there's a place to put that guilt you were talking about, on one of your under-thirties. What's your answer to that?"

"I don't talk to anyone over thirty."

He doesn't know it, but right there we made a pact.

27. GROWING OLDER DISGRACEFULLY

It is always sad to see a man in the prime of life suddenly and perceptibly aging before his time. But on a recent NBC-TV special it was miraculously hilarious to see and hear a thirty-nine-year-old young man confess before millions of viewers that he was that day celebrating his seventy-fifth birthday.

Of course it was Jack Benny, who had been thirty-nine since he was forty. He seemed eager and happy to tell his age to anyone within earshot, as if the burden of his nefarious masquerade had lain heavily upon his conscience for too long.

He even summoned courage to ask a ten-year-old girl on the program how old she thought he was. The child stared thoughtfully into his beaming face bent closely over her, and said, "Oh, I'd say you're about forty or forty-one."

Mr. Benny laughed gleefully at her naïveté. He thanked her but confessed he was really somewhat older, and smilingly encouraged her to guess again. She did, loud and clear.

"Seventy-five," she said.

His smile faded, and he stared at her. And stared. And stared. And the miracle was that Jack Benny, who had been an old thirty-nine, had suddenly become a young seventy-five.

To each his own. Around our house age hasn't been handled that gracefully. Birthdays went out of style some years ago at breakfast when my wife said: "Well, dear, how do you feel this morning on your birthday?"

"Old," I replied.

"Now, dear, that's the wrong altitude."

"Well, Jane, I'm not flying, if that's what you mean."

"No, I mean you keep forgetting what I told you. If I told you once, I told you twice. Don't say you're old, just say you're only getting older. Now repeat after me: I'm not old."

"I'm not old."

"I'm only getting older."

"I'm only getting older."

"Now, don't you feel better? Worry is what makes a person old. I had an aunt whose hair was snow-white. One day she decided not to worry any more, and overnight her hair turned brown. You make it sound as if you're older than Macushla. From now on, we won't mention birthdays around here, if they upset you so. You are not old. You are only getting older. Right?"

"Right. But my glasses are old, and my ears."

"But not you. The word 'birthday' is tatoo around here."

And so with that indelibly inscribed we haven't mentioned or celebrated birthdays for some years. Although the day following that sparkling little chat I did find a package on the dresser. It was a sweater.

"I just happened to accidentally pass a store," she said, "and it was just your shade."

And it was. It was a sort of faded yellow. With a split infinitive. And that's how it's been—the day following every birthday she happened to accidentally pass a store, etc., etc.

That was about ten or twelve sweaters ago. Also, I confess to ten or twelve bottles of White Shoulders perfume from me. No parties, no cakes, no candles to blow out. Just accidentally passing stores through the leisurely flow of time.

And you want to know something? It has taken years off my age. The secret is simple. I pass it on. Follow carefully:

Since birthdays are not my bag any more, I haven't bothered to keep a chronological record. Some time ago, I had a birthday hiatus of three years. Then, I received a Hallmark thing from a sister. That reminded me of the date. So I simply added one year to the number at which I had left off three years before.

After four more years of no birthdays there came a telegram to remind me. But I couldn't remember the number at which I had previously left off. So I selected an attractive, young number, and added one year to that. According to my abacus I am now a sexagenarian.

I like that word. It has a ring to it. A ring of excitement and élan. And, alas, of promise.

She didn't mention my birthday this year. But there was an oblique reference: "I heard a funny joke today about

age," she said. "I hope I can tell it right. Oh yes, I got it:
A man is as old as he looks. A woman is as old as she likes.
Ha, ha, ha."

"You heard that today?"

"Yes, don't you get it, dear?"

"That joke is not old. It's only getting older."

28. MAN ALIVE

From coast to coast our landscape is picturesquely dotted with large patches of real estate bursting in colorful profusion of hyacinth blue, carnation red, lilac purple, shamrock green, calla lily white, and chrysanthemum yellow.

And above this gay, polychromatic effulgence, the air is permeated with fumes of the no-knock octane that once propelled all these gaily colored used cars across the highways of our country.

This is not going to be a piece on Used Car Lots. Those of you who have been paying attention may recall that recently we took up the study of our new social order, where those who are under the age of thirty refuse to talk to anyone over thirty.

This week we take up the plight of men who have, by some secret alchemy, reached sixty-five without loss of efficiency, enthusiasm, vigor, cerebration, or marbles. They are suddenly unemployable.

So it becomes obvious that as the number of sixty-five-year-old retirements accelerates, our country's landscape from coast to coast will very soon be dotted with Used Man Lots.

It has become the fashion in management, as well as in the labor unions, that when a man reaches sixty-five he is automatically and involuntarily retired. Through, finished, kaput, here's your watch, what's your hurry, and see you around some time, old man.

But now, since the under-thirties seem to have decided to forego learning in favor of a life spent in protest and demonstration for the basic freedom of badgering a dean, industry and labor will one day be hard-put to fill the ranks of knowledgeable men needed so desperately in modern business.

Personnel managers will then be off to the Used Man Lots. And where once a buyer looked over the retreads of a Used Car Lot and kicked a tire, he will now look over an old gentleman and kick his shins.

"What's the mileage on this one?"

"Oh, he's been here about five months," replies the Used Man Dealer. "Came in the day after last Christmas —December 26, just like the tag says."

"How fast can he start in cold weather?"

"Remember that Lindsay snow we had? He was out here every day, off and away."

"Got a later model I can see?"

"Yeh, here's one over here. His boss dropped him off only yesterday. One day after he reached sixty-five. Good as new."

"Well, I don't know. In my business I need someone who moves fast—who can stay in the race. And trustworthy. Is he a churchgoer? And have you got one like this in any other color?"

"Hold it, mister. Used Man Lots don't go for that race, creed, and color discrimination."

"He doesn't even have a rearview mirror."

"Yeh, I asked him about that. Said he was only interested in where he's going. Not where he's been."

"And the horn doesn't work."

"That's another thing he told me. Just doesn't like to blow it."

No, no, no. Tear that all up. The subject is too much with us for lame, contrived comedy routines. Poignant letters come fluttering onto this desk too often—as part of this letter from Mr. E. E. Pearson of Philadelphia indicates:

"It is the 'shotgun' nature of current retirement programs which is the worst evil. . . . As the sweep-second hand goes from 11:59 through 12:00 midnight on the date of their sixty-fifth birthdays, men suddenly become 'surplus.' Their fund of information gained through decades of practical experience becomes instantly devalued to zero. The traumatic shock is beyond description. Nor is there any really effective way to prepare for it. . . . Frankly, I suspect that we are involved in a lost cause."

Not at all, Mr. Pearson. Latest insurance statistics lend credence to your cause. Today, a man-child at age one may be expected to live to be sixty-nine. A man who reaches fifty can live to seventy-six. A man of sixty can make seventy-nine. And a man of sixty-five may anticipate living to eighty-one.

Thus, a man involuntarily retired at sixty-five finds himself with sixteen years of life ahead, most of which constitute a loss of valuable manpower. This is the energy, the efficiency, thrown into the junk pile. Or, if you will, into the Used Man Lot.

Even a tree is not retired before its sap has run its course. Is man that much less a creation? If it is true that we are all God's Children, isn't it also true that we are all God's Old Folks?

29. NOW HEAR THIS

To this confused member of the world audience, it seems that the time has come to widen the communications gap. In these days of fast listening, when radio and television are communicating at us in an overwhelming plethora of information, opinion and fact have become indistinguishable.

Of course "a little knowledge is dangerous." (Thomas Huxley.) But the other side of the coin tells it the way it is: "He that hath knowledge spareth his words." (Proverbs 27.)

Too often TV viewers come away from listening to so many talk shows that the food for thought goes through the ear and travels to the brain before the salivary glands can digest the overflowing potpourri.

(Mixed metaphors are par for TV. As witness this generous helping by Governor George Wallace: "These liberals created a Frankenstein. And now their chickens are coming home to roost.")

As an example of our hearing too much and not listening enough, and as a remedy for it, I offer a playlet:

SCENE: *The outer office of a hearing aid consultant. A small office, complete with three or four chairs, and a small table on which is an assortment of various magazines. Make that only copies of Saturday Review, in all of which the Kingsley Double-Crostics have been filled in from Nos. 1642 to 1799. In one of the chairs sits an elderly woman awaiting her appointment. As the curtain rises, a second elderly woman enters. She sits in a chair across from the first woman.*

SECOND WOMAN: Good morning. I guess I got here a little early for my appointment.

FIRST WOMAN: Yes it is, a lovely day. Much warmer than yesterday.

SW: Oh no, I wouldn't dream of taking your turn. I don't mind waiting.

FW: Of course. Here you can have mine. I'm through with it. (*She hands her the copy of Saturday Review.*)

SW: No, thank you. You're very kind. I went off and forgot my glasses.

FW: Yes, they already did the Double-Crostic. They've done it in all of them, more's the pity.

SW: Yes, I will. It is rather warm in here. (*She stands and removes her coat.*)

FW: Oh, that's a very lovely dress.

SW: No, I usually walk over here. I live nearby.

(*The hearing aid consultant enters. He has two hearing aids in his hand. He speaks to the second woman.*)

CONSULTANT: I thought you'd be here a little early. So I got yours ready too.

SW: Yes, it is a lovely day.

C (*to first woman*): And here's yours. Now attach them

and use them for about five minutes, and if they need an adjustment, I'll be back and make them. (*He exits*).

FW: Oh, mine fits perfectly.

SW: Oh, I can hear you so plainly now.

FW: Me too. Aren't these wonderful? I'm sure glad my son told me to come here and get this. He's paying for mine, you know. I'm a widow.

SW: I am too. But my son wouldn't buy me anything. He's too busy being one of those disreputable hippies.

FW: Disreputable! All that the young people want is a better government.

SW: You must be kidding. The way they upset Mr. Daley's convention?

FW: Dick Nixon said . . .

SW: Nixon! Don't tell me you prefer Nixon.

FW: I suppose you prefer that Communist, George Wallace.

SW: Communist! Boy, do you need a hearing aid!
(*The consultant returns.*)

C: How are they, ladies? Can you hear distinctly?

BOTH: They're too loud.

C: Well, I'll take 'em back and adjust 'em. (*He takes the hearing aids. Exits.*)

FW: Honestly, in all my life.

SW: Well, I should think you would. I accept your apology.

FW: Well, that's different. I accept your apology.

SW: I hope he hurries. I haven't had lunch yet.

FW: WHAT?

SW: I HAVEN'T HAD LUNCH YET. I'M GOING OVER TO SCHRAFFT'S.

FW: ME TOO. I EAT THERE ALL THE TIME.

SW: I GO TO THE ONE ON THIRD AVENUE.

FW: HOW NICE! I DO TOO. LET'S GO.

SW: OK. I'M STARVING. (*Consultant returns with hearing aids.*)

c: Ladies, just a moment! You can't get along without these.

FW: I hope they have chicken pie.

SW: Oh no, let's walk; it's only four blocks.

FW: I always sit by the window.

SW: No, no, we'll go Dutch.

(*They laugh gaily and walk out arm in arm.*)

30. ON RUNNING OUT OF GAS

Bureau of Internal Revenue,
Washington, D.C. 20013

Dear Bureau:

Hi there, Bureau. Long time no see—not since 1954. Remember when you called me down to your branch office here in N. Y. to explain a bouquet of telephone call deductions that I had claimed, and we finally reached a friendly compromise where I paid the full amount, plus penalties and interest?

Well, forgive and forget, I always say. Although you can see I haven't entirely forgotten, I must admit you got to me last summer when I read in the newspaper about that little girl in Philadelphia who wrote your department that she had always wanted a pony, and asked if you could stop deducting withholding tax from her daddy's paycheck for one week so he could buy her the pony.

Although you couldn't stop the withholding, the paper

said, your boys at the Philadelphia office pitched in and
bought her a pony. Now that's what I call heart—18 carat
heart.

"I gave him some carrots," the little girl was quoted,
"and he ate them pretty fast." I wept.

Now don't think I'm asking for a pony. They don't allow ponies in the hotel where I live. But what I do want
you fellows to consider is a "Human Depletion Allowance." You know, something like the Oil Depletion Allowance the oil people have. They've had it since 1926—27.5
per cent off their gross income, which, the law says, can
be used in "finding new reserves to replace those that
have been used up or depleted."

Well, have you any idea how depleted I've been getting, sitting here at a typewriter since 1926? Every day I
roll a blank sheet of paper into this machine, stare for
hours at its whiteness, try to dredge up a well of gushing
information, and the depletion that sets in is immeasur-
able.

Okay, I anticipate what you're going to say—you're
going to tell me that oilmen don't always strike oil; that
it takes a lot of sinking of drills, and casings, and what
not, and that down through the years they often come
up with what are known as "dry wells."

Excuse me for laughing. But down through the years
I've done a lot of drilling myself, and have come up dried
and depleted and with a sinking feeling that you wouldn't
believe! That, I insist, is worth at least a 27.5 per cent
allowance off my gross income. To say nothing of the in-
comes of all humans who down through the years have
depleted themselves in the pursuit of life, liberty, and

happiness, and have wound up with the two irrevocables —death and taxes.

Think about a Human Depletion Allowance. Consider it carefully and with compassion, as you did the pony for the little Philadelphia girl. I realize this is an unfortunate time to be asking for less taxation, with all the money our government needs for ABM, MIRV, and SST, to say nothing of sending men to the moon.

I know how important our moon shots are, and how many billions they cost, although I did think that, after the first landing, our President was a little extravagant when he put in a phone call to the moon. And made it person to person. Who else could have answered?

Incidentally, while we're on the phone bit, I think the President could have saved some money had he not acted so hastily when after the West German election he phoned to congratulate the new Chancellor, and got Kurt Kiesinger. That's when he *should* have made it person to person. He could have congratulated the real winner, Willy Brandt.

When I think of those 1954 phone call deductions that your man here at the IRB didn't allow me, I am even further depleted. Don't you consider a human being to be as important as an inanimate oil well? Or to put it another way, don't you believe a human being, after years of contributing to the government coffers, begins to run out of gas? Shouldn't there be a graduated scale of diminishing taxes when he starts depleting?

Let me know what you think. Or better still, when you're in town, let's talk about it over a drink. A pony of brandy? (Ha ha.) I don't suggest you rush pell-mell to the President to ask what he thinks about a Human Depletion Allowance. He's got enough on his mind right now—what with Vietnam, and inflation, and moratoriums, and having to read all those morning papers to learn what the hell Agnew said last night. Wishing you a bountiful Thanksgiving for your horn of plenty, I am, as always, yours.

31. M IS FOR THE BILLION
THINGS SHE GAVE US

*"The great question of the Seventies is: Shall we surren-
der to our surroundings, or shall we make our peace with
nature, and begin to make reparations for the damage we
have done to our air, to our land, and to our water?"*
— PRESIDENT NIXON

"Hello, is that you, Mom?"

"Who is this?"

"Is this Mother Nature?"

"Yes, who's calling?"

"This is a concerned citizen. Our President has asked
us to make peace with Nature. Can we set up a meeting
where we can sit down and negotiate a peace treaty to
clean up our polluted air, land, and water?"

"OK. But I insist on a hexagonal table."

"Hexagonal? Is that a symbol or something?"

"That'll do for a starter. Count 'em yourself. Six: auto
exhausts, cigarette butts, oil slicks, garbage, chimney
stacks, and gum wrappers."

"Aw, now, Mom, you're being a little intransigent. The shape of the table doesn't matter. I'm a serious, concerned citizen."

"Yeh? What country?"

"America."

"America, huh? Make that table heptagonal. Beer cans."

"Mom. I'm calling long distance. You don't sound as if you're worried about your children down here."

"Just a minute, son. You sound like you think I'm responsible for the mess you're living in. I've been doing my bit. Don't I hang out the sun every morning and the moon at night? And while I'm hanging up the moon, you're throwing out the garbage. You say you're concerned. Just how concerned are you? If you can't get your chimneys to stop smoking, would you stop smoking and contaminating the land with cigarette butts?"

"Well, yes, I would if everyone else stopped smoking. But I refuse to withdraw unilaterally. And besides, if everybody threw away their cigarette packs simultaneously, it would make a mountain of trash up to the moon."

"And your people certainly left a lot of your garbage up there, too. I'm still busy sweeping that under the Milky Way."

"A mother's work is never done."

"What's a mother to do? The air I send down there every day is pure nitrogen and oxygen, in ratio of about four to one. I make a fresh batch every morning, with a few spoonfuls of harmless additives like argon, neon, helium, and krypton. So don't blame me if you dumb people keep adding bottlefuls of sulphur dioxide."

"OK, we'll put that on the agenda. It's a bargaining point. So how about having our peace meeting?"

"Well, I don't know. You caught me at a busy time, a few weeks before spring."

"You have to plant your spring flowers?"

"No, I've done that. I've got to get my April showers hose connected, and move that stupid sun closer to the vernal point, and make a green mix for those summer leaves, and I'm in the middle of putting up jars of bronze dyes for the autumn."

"Oh, I realize you're a busy housekeeper, and the world is your dustbin, but we have a priority problem. We're told that in ten years this world won't be habitable if pollution isn't stopped. So let's have this meeting right away. We should be able to get this foul air and water cleaned up in a week with your cooperation."

"A week! Listen, I'm Mother Nature, not Mother Superior."

"Hahaha. That's very funny, Mom."

"I'm not trying to be funny. I understand your pollution problem, and I guess we should have a meeting."

"Sure, because once we get the pollution out of the way, we have to solve our population explosion."

"Just a minute, boy. Are you against the natural birth of a child?"

"Oh, no, I'm not knocking motherhood."

"Because if population's on the agenda, no peace meeting."

"We won't bring it up. Reminds me of the story about the panicky mother who called the doctor: 'Hurry right over, our six-year-old son just swallowed a birth control pill. Come immediately.' And the doctor said, 'Be calm.

He'll be all right. I'll be there in an hour.' And she said, 'Please hurry.' Then fifteen minutes later she called the doctor again and said, 'You don't have to come over, Doctor. We just found another one.'—Hello?—Hello?"

She hung up. How can you make peace with a crabby dame like that?

32. LIBERTÉ, EGALITÉ, AND MATERNITÉ

If a mere male still retains his right to vote, my vote goes for the liberation of women. If women insist on equal pay for equal jobs, I say give it to them. And God bless.

What I don't understand is why women, no matter how highly qualified, want equal opportunity for promotion to the high executive jobs now held by men. I hate to be a spoilsport, but if women are under the impression that by rosalindrusselling it in a big executive suite, they will add to their lives, I beg them to read the latest vital statistics pamphlet issued by the insurance companies.

A male's life expectancy, it states, is 67.0. A female can live to the ripe old age of 74.2. Although the Declaration of Independence proclaims all men to have been created equal, somewhere along the way the male has lost 7.2 years of life to the female.

Any physician will tell you (if you go to his office; they don't make house calls any more) that male executives—pushing and being pushed around in the market place, being hounded by competitors bent on taking the food out of the mouths of their children or the minks off the backs of their wives, or awaking a sleeping ulcer when the big boss doesn't say "good morning" in the office hall—will find their life spans shortened to 67.0.

On the other hand, there is the unliberated woman, whose hands are busy vacuuming as she watches *As the World Turns* on TV, who has to experiment with blue and white detergents on the family wash, who has to make certain her furniture polish has enough lemon in it, and who phones the grocer to ask why he didn't credit her with 6 cents for the three empty Coke bottles—this woman will statistically attain the age of 74.2.

One cannot but admire a woman who, for the sake of equality with men, is willing to give up 7.2 years of her life. The obvious reasoning is that it's a small price to pay to obliterate man's image of women as sex pots, pussycats, second-class citizens, and *Playboy* centerfolds with stapled chests.

To dramatize their demands, thousands of women recently marched down Fifth Avenue in New York. In the interest of research I went over to follow along. It was, for the most part, a peaceful and happy demonstration.

It got out of hand for a moment, however, when several men heckled insultingly, and some of the girls went at them tooth and manicure. This seemed unseemly to me, who thinks that women should always be ladies. Or at least be gentlemen.

The march wound up at a park, and I listened to speeches of the leaders. I was won over by the logic of most, but confused by Betty Friedan, organizer of the National Organization for Women, who said: "Men are not our enemy, but the kind of society men have constructed is."

That's pure feminine logic, if you'll pardon my giving logic a gender. It's like one woman gushing to another: "I have a secret I can't tell. Not that I think you'll tell it to anyone, but the people you tell it to might tell it."

Nevertheless, women are off to a grand start. In due time, they will be seated in upper-level, lavish, penthouse offices, making like high executives. Now, I hate to get back to this gnawing worry, ladies, but here's how it's going to work out that you lose your extra 7.2 years of expectancy. Life expectancy, of course.

Chasing a handsome, young, male junior executive around your lavish private office takes a lot of running. That will easily take off 2.3 years.

Having your secretary burst into your office without knocking and finding that junior executive on your lap will knock off another 1.1 years.

Taking out an important, big-money client in Manhattan to dine and drink, and having him insist you take him downtown to the Off-Broadway production of *Oh! Calcutta!* will subtract another 1.2 years.

Having an after-theater nightcap in a nightclub, then pouring him into his hotel room at 2 in the morning, and maneuvering to escape a fate worse than death will check off another 2.6 years of life.

Don't bother adding it. I've done it for you. But with no male chauvinism. I know women can add and subtract, as well as multiply.

It all comes out to a shorter life span. But just between us men, ladies, a merrier one. Right? Even that one junior executive up there beats looking for that lemon in all those bottles of furniture polish.

33. SENIOR CITIZENS LIB MOVEMENT

OK. The women have fought the good fight to demonstrate, they are not to be considered mere telephone operators, typists, mannequins, or, God forbid, the lovable possessions of men. In particular, Women's Lib has ad-libbed brilliantly and successfully in its crusade for day-care services for children.

But now it is time to turn to another nervous group of second-class citizens: the elderly who are fighting for more day- and night-care nursing homes for the aged and struggling for a haven during the time of life that is euphemistically referred to as "When you reach December."

A cruel metaphor. Men and women, aged seventy, would be better served, and better able to cope with the frightening and eroding processes, if they were referred to as having reached September. Psychologically, they could better survive if they have reached October at eighty, November at ninety, and December at 100. In January they are on their own.

At age seventy, eighty, or ninety, no woman is provided with a grandmother sitter. Granny and/or Granddaddy are accused of the heinous offense of growing old, coughing hackingly, hardening their arteries, failing in their hearing, and harboring cataracts.

They have been judged by a jury of their relative peers and found guilty of intent to grow old in the first degree. They have been shunted off to overcrowded and undertended homes for the old, if there is space. That's the plight of our senior citizens.

In contrast, for our freshman citizens, aged one to five, more day-care centers are sprouting everywhere. Thanks in measure to Women's Lib, the tots are winning their revolution. Happy and carefree, they are spending their young age in comforting and salubrious group therapy.

That they are flourishing and growing mentally is manifest by the overwhelming number of clever sayings attributed to little kids. They are forever, and tiresomely, being quoted in the press and in books. "Out of the mouths of babes," the belief is, "come words of great wisdom and sparkling wit." No four- or five-year-old ever tells a humorless joke. That's a lot of Pablum! Who do they think they are? No baby was ever President of the United States—or even president of a bankrupt railroad.

There are sluggards in all age groups. In first childhood and in second childhood. Infants aren't born with a gift for comedy. I have known four- and five-week-olds who couldn't adlib a burp after a bottle of formula without being savagely pummeled on the back. As for those who, now and then, do come up with a big yak, I'm of the opinion that they have writers.

The monologist Sam Levenson has made a career out

of the funny things children are said to have said. And
with no residuals to the kids. The other day I heard Mr.
Levenson tell the one about a little boy who had lost his
mother at an airport and asked a baggage handler: "Did
you see a woman walking around here without a kid that
looks like me?" OK, if Mr. Levenson can come up with
the kid who said that, I can get that tike a job on
Laugh-In.

Now what about the old folks? Are they to be seen and
not heard? To get a better public image, and to start a
vigorous crusade for more and better homes for the aged,
the oldsters should begin a program to call attention to
the humorous things *they* say, which will also make them
cute and cuddly. A public relations man could have their
sparks of humor mimeographed and distributed.

Like the little old lady I heard about who went to her
doctor for her annual checkup.

"You are in good shape," he said "for a woman of your
age. How old are you now, my dear?"

"I am one hundred and two years old," she replied.

"One hundred and two! Amazing! You are in extraor-
dinary shape."

"Thank you, doctor. I'll see you next year."

"I hope so. You sound very confident."

"I am. I looked up the statistics," she said, "and I found
that very few women die between one hundred and two
and one hundred and three."

If it works for little children, it will work for old folks.
We live in times of revolution. No section of the citizenry
has failed to demonstrate for the goals it seeks.

Arise, old-timers of the world! But slowly. Throw off
your shackles, your canes, your shawls, and, if possible,

your glasses. Demonstrate! But peacefully! March in a proud parade down Fifth Avenue. A short parade. Say, from 57th Street to 55th Street. We don't want anyone tiring, do we?

And Thensome

Consisting of Flotsam and Jetsam

34. OH, SAY CAN'T YOU SEE?

I'm as proud of our flag and the Republic for which it stands, one nation under God, indivisible, as is the next taxi driver. But this one was bent on giving me a hard time.

I did not start the debate. Since we are a "nation indivisible," I try to keep it that way. So I don't start anything with cabbies. He started it when he pointed to a six-inch flag that hung from the inside of his windshield.

Before I relate the actual conversation, I want to take the oath that I am a loyal, patriotic American who believes it is the right of anyone to express his fervent patriotism by displaying a flag. But if his purpose is to demonstrate that I'm less of an American than he, I resent it. OK?

"I had to buy a new flag," my man said. "Some long-haired hippie must have swiped it last night when I went in for a cup of coffee. So I had to buy a new one. Too much disrespect for Old Glory going around these days."

"I know what you mean," I said. "So you're flying a New Glory today. But it's too bad you don't have your flag hanging on a staff."

"A staff? How'm I gonna get a staff on this windshield? What difference does it make?"

"Well, according to the flag code," I said, "a flag should not be displayed on a float, or a motor vehicle, or a boat, unless it's on a staff."

"Who said that?"

"It's the flag code," I replied, taking it out of my pocket, where I carry it for such occasions next to my American Express card. "This flag code for civilian display of the flag," I continued, "was passed by Congress in 1942."

"Yeh? And I'll bet you that those Congressmen were soft on long-haired hippies."

Rather than get into a discourse on his anachronistic hippies of 1942, I tried to drop the subject. But he wasn't dissuaded.

"I wear a flag pin on my lapel too," he said, turning around to show it. "Like every true American should," he added, staring at my nude lapel.

"I'm sorry," I apologized. "I left it on the suit I wore last night," I lied. "But does that make me a good American last night, and a disloyal American today?"

"No, I wouldn't go that far. But in these times when everybody's picking on us and trying to start a war with us, we gotta let 'em know we're for America night and day."

"By the way," I said, not knowing enough to keep my mouth shut, "the flag code says that the flag should be flown only from sunrise to sunset. Do you take your flag pin in every evening at sunset?"

He sat up and stared at me in his rear-view mirror. I gave him my friendliest smile. Who knows? He might have been tempted to make a citizen's arrest. But the smile got him.

"That's very funny," he laughed. "But there's nothing funny about our flag, mister. All Americans have been proud of it since good old Betsy Ross sewed up the first Stars and Stripes."

"I beg your pardon," I said, going full steam ahead, "but Betsy Ross did not sew up the first flag. That's a legend no historian has been able to prove."

Just sitting there, he grew two inches taller, and I realized we were not flying united. A little music might clear the atmosphere.

"Do you know the song that goes with the flag, 'The Star-Spangled Banner'?" I asked.

"Sure. I sing it every time I go to a ball game," and he proceeded to sing: "Oh, say can you see by the dawn's early light what so proudly we hailed at the twilight's last gleaming? And the rocket's red glare . . ."

"You left out 'Whose broad stripes.'"

"Oh yes. Whose broad stripes and bright stars, through the perilous night . . ."

"Fight," I corrected.

"You sure?"

"That's it."

"OK," he said continuing. "Over the ramparts we watched were so gallantly streaming. And the rocket's red glare, the planes bursting in air . . ."

"Excuse me," I interrupted. "I get out here. But you should hear this from me rather than from a stranger. It's 'bombs bursting in air.' When Francis Scott Key wrote the song, there were no planes. Anyway, you sing real fine; here's a dollar tip for it. And don't forget to enter that as income when you make out your federal tax return."

"What are you, FBI?"

"No, just a loyal, patriotic American."

"Boy, it takes all kinds!"

35. MORE BLESSED TO GET THAN TO GIVE

Have you ever been invited to a dog fight? Has anyone ever phoned and said, "Hey, there's a good dog fight at the Garden tonight. I have four seats. Would you and Jane join Mae and me for dinner, and then we'll go to the dog fight"?

Ring a bell? No? Well, then maybe you can tell me why, whenever I bring home some small gift—a scarf, a pair of gloves—my wife says, "Thank you very much for thinking of me, dear, but I wouldn't wear a thing like this to a dog fight."

In all our married, harried years I have never considered, or even dreamed of, dragging her to a dog fight. I have taken her to the theater, to movies, to ballgames, to the opera. But I have never, I beseech you to believe me, NEVER suggested taking her to a dog fight.

She has some lovely, appropriate things to wear to places we do go. She bought those herself. But whenever I buy her something, there is this obsession that lurks in her subconscious (if you'll pardon the four-letter word) mind that I have been scurrying through department stores to find her something she *would* wear to a dog fight. For heavens sake, I don't even know what the well-dressed woman is supposed to wear to a dog fight.

Against that background, you're wondering why I continue to buy her these small gifts. They're not anniversary or birthday remembrances. They have to do with this hang-up of mine: Every time I buy a shirt or a tie for myself I feel an oppressive guilt that sends me buying something for her to compensate for my extravagance.

Stupid, isn't it? But interesting, as any psychiatrist would tell me after a year or two of thrashing around on his upholstery while he tried to rid me of this mania, at a cost of $50 a forty-five-minute hour, which used to be fifty-five minutes at $40. While analysts' prices have been inflated by $10, they compensate by deflating the hour by ten minutes. I wonder who works out their guilt pangs.

It was an especially pangy guilt that hit me the other day in a department store when I fingered a tie on a counter. I held it at my throat, and a saleswoman hollered for all to hear, "That tie is twenty dollars."

She thought I would drop it. So did I. But I didn't.

"Who asked you how much it was?" I said. "Don't I look like a twenty-dollar-tie man to you? Besides, haven't you heard the old saying that if you have to ask the price of a tie, you can't afford it?"

"Yes, I have," she replied.

"No, you haven't," I said. "I just made that up. The old saying is what J. P. Morgan said, that if you have to ask the price of a yacht, you can't afford it."

"Do you want the tie or not?" she said.

"Yes," I chickened. "Wrap it up."

I paid in cash. She wasn't going to identify me by credit card as a man she and I were both sure would drop a $20 tie when he heard the price.

Twenty dollars for a tie is ridiculous. Especially this wide, wide tie she palmed off on me. Wide, wide $20 ties completely cover $30 shirts, which are completely covered by $150 double-breasted, high-buttoned jackets, which cover the frames of men who live in thrall to dictates of busybody fashion designers and who are too weak to halt the inflation spiral.

Well that was the day of the Big Guilt. After a $20 tie, a scarf or a pair of gloves would not assuage the pang. I went immediately to the mink coat department . . . then to the mink jackets . . . then to cloth coats . . . and finally settled on a quilted bedjacket.

As I handed her the package I said, "Jane, please don't say you wouldn't wear this to a dog fight."

She opened it. "Thank you very much for thinking of me, dear. . . ."

"But you wouldn't wear it to a dog fight?"

"I love it."

"Then I finally bought you something you *would* wear to a dog fight."

"Why do you keep barking on a dog fight? If you buy me things because you're under the impersonation that I want to go to a dog fight, then you know what I've got half a mind?"

"Well, yes, but I've never put it in so many words."

"I've got half a mind to send this back. Besides, I wouldn't wear anything to a dog fight."

"Jane, I think you've been seeing too many movies." Etc., etc.

36. THE CHOO-CHOO BUSINESS

If you think you are having money problems, consider the plight of the Penn Central Transportation Company, the largest railroad system in the country. It has gone into bankruptcy.

Like the rest of us, Penn Central has been driven off its trolleys trying to make both ends meet. It may lighten your burden to read some figures. Briefly, last year Penn Central lost $100-million on its passenger service. This year, despite a new president who took over running the railroad at $250,000 a year, the company has lost in the first three months $62.7-million. And there are some small debt issues that annually cost the company $95-million in interest.

All those figures may be beyond your ken, but they are only figures of speech—that is, figures that are spoken more glibly than they are read. Nevertheless, it is my educated guess that things at Penn Central are not going too well.

It demonstrates two points: that Penn Central is only

human, and that those charge plates can get anyone into a lot of trouble. But before you suggest that Penn Central apply for welfare, you have to look at the whole picture—in black and red.

Penn Central owns several blocks of real estate on Park Avenue that are worth $7-billion. So you see, *on* Park Avenue Penn Central is doing very well. It's *under* Park Avenue where the trains run that Penn Central is in a hole.

Also, Penn Central is showing a profit on its hauling of freight. Freight is doing very well, and the company is never bothered with complaints from freight about having to wait out there on a siding somewhere for a train to come lagging along. However, the profit from freight is not nearly sufficient to make up for the yearly $100-million the road loses on passengers.

In everyday jargon, it's like the corner drugstore that loses money on its medical supplies and tooth pastes, but makes money at its fountain on tuna fish sandwiches and toasted bagels. If the fountain business doesn't do well enough to cover the losses on the other items, the corner drugstore goes into bankruptcy.

But the kind of bankruptcy for the corner drugstore is different from that facing Penn Central. Under Section 77 of the Bankruptcy Law, the railroad goes into what is known as "reorganization." The trains continue in business, and creditors have to wait and hope for some future day, or year, when Penn Central is solvent enough to pay its bills.

When the corner drugstore goes into bankruptcy, it goes out of business, and a sheriff or somebody sells all the unused tooth paste and tuna fish to pay off the cred-

itors immediately, and our poor little druggist is left with
the hole in his toasted bagel.

If I sound against the Establishment, I'm not. It's not
my nature or my age bracket. I admire big business people who look for loopholes. I'm always looking for them.
I never find them, but I keep looking.

Actually, I do find them, but my legal adviser always
finds a loophole in my loopholes. He has a great lawyer
mind, having studied under *Judd for the Defense* for two
years and having taken a refresher course during the summer reruns of Perry Mason.

As an old railroad man myself, I empathize with Penn
Central. It was at the age of six that I acquired a steel
locomotive made of tin, and two freight cars, which ran
across a wall-to-wall carpet in the home of my parents,
with whom I was living at the time.

My freight cars hauled coal. Since I had no passenger
service, I was operating a railroad at a profit. Until my
father discovered one day that our coal bin was slowly
being depleted. I was losing coal enroute across the room,
and my mother felt it was damaging her carpet.

Between the two, I was forced into Section 77 of the
Bankruptcy Law, twenty years before President Herbert
Hoover even thought of signing Section 77.

Under the reorganization, I went back to my roller
skates and to spinning my top. It has been spinning ever
since.

Penn Central must feel relieved that its sorrowful
plight is out in the open. A great railroad to be down at
its wheels is not a thing one suffers in privacy. This is a
time for friends. We are all friends of Penn Central. Its re-

organization will be like the opening of a window to let some fresh air in on its troubles and to solve them.

If, of course, there is anyone around who knows how to open a Penn Central window.

37. ACCENTUATE THE MINIMUM; ELIMINATE THE MAXIMUM

We can all learn a lesson about budget cutting from our President. When they handed him the final figures that showed a balanced 1970-71 budget plus a small surplus, he turned to his assembled Cabinet, the newspapers report, and said, "We've got to do even better."

When I looked at the final figures of the bills I received in January, I turned to my assembled Wife and said, "We've got to do even better."

"Better than what?" she asked.

"Better than all these bills."

"Oh, that's last month's. Wait till you see how I saved sixty dollars on this month's bills."

"How did you do that? I'm afraid to ask."

"Wait, I'll show you."

She returned entirely submerged in one of those new maxi coats.

"How do you like it? Isn't it stunning? I think it's stunning. It was on sale from $170 to $110. I think it's stunning. Doesn't it to you?"

If a man answers that question truthfully, it's an invitation to a declaration of war. A maxi coat on a mini wife is not the most ravishing sight in the world. So, diplomat that I am, I phrased my critique as kindly as I could.

"Take it back," I said.

That had one desired effect. She was momentarily speechless. I took advantage of that moment.

"Jane, our President has spent many sleepless nights trying for a balanced budget. He made cuts everywhere to help stop inflation. And it behooves all citizens to follow his example. Besides, I don't like the coat on you. You're lost in it. I don't like those maxis on anybody."

"But the maxi is the latest style. And it's warm from head to toe. Besides, I thought you'd be happy I saved sixty dollars. It's a good buy."

"I hate long good buys."

"Beg pardon?"

"Let's forget about the style. The President is making cuts in his budget; the least we can do is to make cuts too. Take it back. Your cooperation will warm the cockles of our President's heart."

"Oh sure, his. But how about *my* cockles—freezing out there in this cold weather? Don't they matter to you?"

"You've got other coats, Jane. The idea is to cut down spending so much money."

"Money!" she shouted. "Who spent money? I charged it."

"I'm glad you said that. That is the solution. You have just spoken the words that trigger the very wellspring of vicious inflation."

"I did not. All I said was—"

"You charged it. Your credit card is at the root of inflation. A woman at a department store stands undecided, weighing a twenty-five-dollar bag in one hand, a hundred-dollar bag in the other. Which should she buy? She finally decides, 'Oh well, I don't have to pay money, I can charge it. I'll take the hundred-dollar one.' Now, if there were a law passed by Congress that buying with credit cards should be treated like buying a stock at a broker's office—which requires a 70 per cent margin—this woman would never shell out seventy dollars and charge the other thirty. Do you get what I'm driving at?"

"You're right. I should have charged a bag to go with my maxi."

"Jane, you're not cooperating with our President. He's trying so hard to bring our budget into balance. Our country has to be strong economically. If it isn't, he won't be able to deal properly with Vietnam, the Middle East, Health, Education and Welfare, the moon program, mass transportation, and the polluted air and water that threaten our very survival."

"You mean, all that depends on my maxi coat?"

"Yes, you and a million other short women."

"Well, I'll think about it," she said.

To guide her thinking I came home the next day with a purchase of my own—one of those new jackets, wide lapels, tight fitting, with more buttons than you'll find on an accordion, and with a flare you wouldn't believe. I modeled it.

"Isn't it stunning?" I asked.

"Take it back," she said.

"Why? Is the jacket too hippie?"

"No, but you are. And it's not your style. You're too uh—"

"Tall?" I asked.

"No, that's not the word. Too uh—"

"Too short?"

"No, that's not the word."

"Too old?"

"That's the word. I'll tell you what, dear—if you take yours back, I'll take mine back."

"Now you're talking, Jane. The President will be proud of your sacrifice. You are now a member of the Silent Majority."

"And the cold majority."

38. NO ONE TO TALK TO

Last August, I went into a new business. I made myself available to a booking agency for the lecture circuit. This has been the best-kept secret in all show biz. I head the list of Ten Least Wanted Speakers.

How I got involved was, one day I was on the phone with an associate at *Saturday Review* who suggested I go on the road and give some talks to readers of this magazine at clubs, universities, luncheons, and dinners to find out what they're thinking and talking about.

"It'll be educational for you and enjoyable. Some of our editors are doing it," he said. "I'll call the W. Colston Leigh agency and have them get in touch with you."

"Yes," I said, "we must do that one day."

Well, one day turned out to be one minute after I hung up. Mr. Leigh was on the phone and said he'd like to come over to talk about it. He came with a contract which I signed on August 19, making myself available. I immediately got ahead on my other work to make time for all those speeches I was to make on my road tour.

Three months later, on November 15, I heard from

Mr. Leigh. He had made a contract for my first booking.

"Well, finally," I said. "Where is it, Mr. Leigh?"

"Gloversville, New York."

"Good. When is it?"

"On a Saturday night."

"Good. Is that this week or next?"

"January 11," he replied.

Well, anyone can easily see that any bee was going to be a lot busier than I. Is this the famous Chautauqua circuit I had heard so much about? Is this the way William Jennings Bryan got started?

I had never spoken in public before, and despite what you may have read, I cannot talk off the top of my head. But I kept saying that with two whole months to go I had plenty of time before old January 11 rolled around.

But old January 11, as all January 11s do, rolled around sooner than expected. Still no speech. However, I had reservations on a train, and the three-and-a-half-hour ride would give me the time needed.

Strangely enough it was my wife who gave me an opening line. I hadn't mentioned this new kick I was on to Jane, but I had to explain because on Saturdays we go to a Broadway matinee.

"I won't be able to make the theater with you today," I said as I left, "so you better round up someone to go with."

"Why?" she asked. "Where are you going this early?"

"I'm going up to Gloversville, New York, to make a speech," I replied.

And she said, "All right, then don't tell me."

I made a note to open with that. The train left at 8:30. I

settled back with pen and pad, and at 8:35 I was sound
asleep. At 12, I was awakened by the conductor.

Gloversville was covered with snow. Its landscape was
wintry picturesque. In the crisp, clean air, trees stood
leafless against a cold blue sky, their fingers reaching
glovelessly up into the icy winds.

But the people were warm and hospitable, their response intelligent and instantaneous. The subject was television, a peek behind the scenes, a sort of thumbnose
description of my life through the years in service of the
stars for whom I had written. I was amazed at the sound
of clear, honest, uncanned laughter. They seemed to
be getting even with their TV sets at home.

Wouldn't you think, this January date being my first
outing, Mr. Leigh would have sent someone to monitor
the speech? No one. I got to the office early Monday to
await his call. None came Monday. Or Tuesday or
Wednesday. On Thursday I sent Mr. Leigh a note: "I'm
sorry about what happened in Gloversville. All I can say
is that it wasn't my fault."

That would make him call. Nothing Monday, Tuesday,
Wednesday. On Thursday, January 23, I couldn't stand
it. I phoned him.

"Hi," he said. "I just saw your note here about something that happened in Gloversville. What happened?"

"It's too delicate to discuss on the phone," I replied.

"I don't know what it could have been. I have their
check here. And I have another booking for you."

Well, that was more like it. I perked up. "Where?"

"Cincinnati."

"When?"

"October."

Slave driver!

39. HEY, TAXI

I am the worst cab-getter in the whole world, and that includes rickshas in China.

The title was bestowed by my wife the other night as we huddled with several other Manhattanites under a restaurant canopy on a snow-swept street. She had just watched three men commandeer three cabs right off my finger tips and rescue their wives from the freezing cold.

"You are the worst cab-getter in the whole world, including gin rickeys in China," she proclaimed in a brief eulogistic ceremony.

As I knelt in the snow to be knighted, I murmured, "There's quite a crowd here, and those three men were ahead of us."

"You couldn't even get a cab," she replied, "if you were on the moon with only those three astronauts on it."

"There were only two on the moon."

"That's worse yet," she retorted. "I know you can't whistle through your teeth like everybody else can [I can't], but the way to get a cab is to give the doorman a tip."

"There's no doorman here."

"Excuses, excuses."

A few days later she made the award official by presenting me with a tiny solid gold whistle.

"Here," she said, "is a tiny solid gold whistle that you can whistle to get a cab. It's really to put on your charm bracelet, but you don't wear one; so you can hook it on to your key ring." I hooked it on.

I must admit again that I am not one of your most aggressive cab-getters. I have been beaten out of cabs by a sixty-year-old woman, a seventy-five-year-old man, a 36-22-36 young lady, and a forty-six-inch boy. As for the three men under the canopy that night, they were absolutely members of the Oakland Raiders.

William Powell—remember him in *The Thin Man?* Now, there was a talented cab-getter. I admired and envied him every time he and Myrna Loy came out of their apartment. No sooner had William Powell reached the curb and raised a gloved hand than a cab pulled up.

And when they got to the restaurant where they were to dine, that was sheer magic. In one beautiful orchestrated motion, he handed the cabbie the fare, and he and Myrna swept suavely into the restaurant.

Now me. We come out of the apartment, I almost get a cab, when some guy a few feet ahead of me darts out from nowhere and grabs it.

"You almost had it," she says. "When you let that man get your cab you could have knocked me down with a fender." I am sorely tempted.

When we arrive at the restaurant, she's always sitting near the door through which we have to exit; so I have to crawl over her to help her out. My hat falls off; my posture is definitely not William Powell; it's more Lon Chaney in *The Hunchback of Notre Dame*.

Then, fumbling for the fare, I discover the smallest bill I have is a ten spot, and the cabbie wants to know if I think he's a bank; so I run across the street to get change in a cigar store, which the man resents until I buy some pipe tobacco, that I don't smoke, and I hustle back to gather up my bride, and we sweep into the restaurant in one discordant motion.

After we are seated, she says sarcastically, "Well, do you still feel like William Powell?"

"No," I reply tartly, "I feel more like Guy Lombardo on New Year's morning. And I'm sure Myrna Loy would never have made a crack like that to him."

"Myrna Loy was never married to Guy Lombardo. You've got your couples mixed."

It was the very next day that she presented me with that tiny solid gold whistle I had hooked to my key ring. That afternoon I was in the snow, without her at my elbow, waiting for a cab. I decided to test my whistle.

I stood off the curb in the street and blew it. What can I tell you? Only a dog could have heard it. A small dog nestled in your arms close to your cheek. I huffed and I puffed, but it did not attract any cab driver.

But it did attract a police car, with two burly cops. As I kept blowing, they watched me suspiciously.

"Hey, Mac," one of them called out, "why are you blowing on your key ring?"

"Oh," I replied, "I'm not blowing on my key ring. You

see, I'm the worst cab-getter in the world. So my wife gave me this tiny solid gold whistle to blow for a cab."

"Isn't that darling?" he said to his partner.

"The woods are full of 'em," he said.

40. HOW TO CANCEL A MAGAZINE
AND GET TWO IN ITS PLACE

It occurred to me a year ago that I was overread. It was the night I was in bed, having tuned the TV set to Channel 3—no program there, but it gives a soft light to read by. I was leafing through a book, when the phone rang.

I reached down to answer it, poking through the unread material that had piled up around the bedside table —stacks of magazines, books, clippings, pamphlets, galley proofs, a ruler, yellow scratch pads, an assortment of pens and heavy pencils, brochures, a pot of glue, and a large pair of shears. And there was the phone.

"City desk," I barked.

That was when I realized somebody would have to clean up this mess. And it would have to be I, because of this note to the maid I had printed in big block letters on a shirt cardboard: DON'T DISTURB.

My intentions had been the noblest. I had to be informed. For heaven's sake, this was research for all my readers out there. It was just that my mind was larger than my eyes. There had been several complaints from the lady of the house. I explained it was my 57th Street annex of the Public Library. Her descriptions of my Storehouse of Knowledge contained such unfriendly references as "junk yard," "city dump," "fire hazard," and that old classic, "not worth the paper it's written on."

To get rid of this plethora of printed words, I spent the weekend throwing out some of the accumulation. The pot of glue went first, followed by the large shears, the scratch pad, and the newspaper clippings of the first landing on the moon that I had been saving as a sort of Cook's Tour guide if I ever decided to travel there.

But it was the magazines that required the Big Decision. Many of them would have to be canceled. But I decided to make it a gradual withdrawal. Two the first six months, then two more, and hopefully I could see the light at the end of the tunnel by 1972.

I began the de-escalation with one of my favorite magazines, which I shall call *The Old Yorker*. It had been coming to the apartment for many years. The subscription still had a year to go; so I decided to transfer the balance of the subscription to a nephew living in Prairie Village, Kansas.

At my office the next day, I wrote a letter to the magazine directing the transfer, and sent it with my office address. That was a big mistake.

The following week I got a card at the office addressed to Mrs. Ace. The card read: "We acknowledge with thanks your Christmas gift subscription order." Which is more than I got from my nephew, who began receiving *The Old Yorker*. Which is understandable, because it wasn't anywhere near Christmas.

Why they thanked Mrs. Ace I don't know, because she knew nothing about it. I don't think she even knows where the office is. But I was glad to be out of it. This was to be her problem, if I ever tell her about it. But now the office was being cluttered with more of her mail.

The following week a copy of *The Old Yorker* came to the office addressed to Mrs. Ace, computer number 58004 00385094 50069 2 X. Which I thought was a pretty good description. That computer had her number all right.

As copies of *The Old Yorker* started piling up in gay profusion at the office, another letter came to Mrs. Ace, reminding her that her subscription was about to expire. I wasn't sure which subscription they meant, the one she was getting here that she hadn't subscribed to, or the subscription I had transferred to Prairie Village, Kansas. To play safe, I renewed the Kansas subscription.

To double check, I phoned my nephew. Yes, he was getting it. He loved *The Old Yorker,* and he thanked me effusively.

"You're welcome," I said. "I just renewed your subscription for another year."

His response to that bit of news was something less than gracious.

"For heaven's sake," he said, "why did you do that? Our bedroom is getting cluttered up with so many magazines I can't even find the phone!"

P.S.: I know what you're thinking. But this piece is not an invitation for letters about the computer problems you may be having with *Saturday Review.* Like this letter to me from Wichita from Doctor and Mrs. 47D E67200W-NC4 BLO31995SR2. From that number, you sound like nice people. Better think again before canceling your subscription just because your copies have been delayed a bit. You'll get only two instead of one.

41. WITH HER IN THE HOUSE, WHO NEEDS TELEVISION?

This is being written at the behest of a friend named Jane Doe. She asked me not to divulge her true identity. ("Just sign it Unanimous," she said.)

Jane Doe is one of the wealthiest and most powerful women in America. Among her vast holdings are 112 shares of AT&T, which she has secretly acquired over the years, and which includes several stock splits. ("Look, dear, my AT&T had babies.")

She began throwing her power around the other evening when I read to her from the newspaper that the Equal Employment Opportunity Commission had brought drastic charges against AT&T for its hiring practices in the matter of sex.

"Sex!" she said, bolting upright. "They're blaming AT&T for all those obscene phone calls?"

"Of course not. They claim AT&T is not giving women equal job opportunity with men."

"That's a bald-headed lie, and I want you to write that in your magazine. You can tell 'em about Annie and the job I got her at the telephone company."

"Annie? I don't seem to recall—"

"Annie was that beautiful waitress at the tearoom where we used to have lunch every day who told us she was quitting her job because she wasn't getting enough tips."

"Oh, of course. Annie, the tipless waitress."

"That's the one. First, I thought I'd get her into the movies, she's so pretty. I have sixty shares of Metro-Goldwyn-Mayer. I called a man at the movie company, and I wrote several letters to him telling him about my stock."

"I didn't know you did that."

"Well, I wanted to surprise you when she became a movie star. I wrote him that Annie's so beautiful she would be a really big box-office draw."

"And what happened?"

"Well, I got her the job, but she didn't like the hours of being a cashier in a box office."

"A big box-office draw, yes."

"So then I called the phone company. I have a connection there too—with my hundred and twelve shares."

"Big deal."

"Oh, yes, I told them she wanted to work for AT&T, and they gave her a job. I'll bet she's the most beautiful telephone operator there."

"I don't recall her being all that beautiful."

"She has beautiful blond hair, and big blue eyes, and a cute little nose, and her mouth goes without saying."

"At the switchboard of the phone company, of course."

"Yes, now you write in your magazine that they gave her a job and that it proves they're not unfair about giving a job to someone who happens to be a woman."

"But, Jane, that's what women are objecting to—why should they be considered only for jobs as telephone operators?"

"Because a telephone operator means a woman. You never hear anybody say, 'The operator, he cut me off.' They always say, 'She cut me off.' Telephone operator is a feminine noun. Like receptionist. Everybody knows a receptionist is a pretty girl. So is a nurse, or a manicurist."

"Or a belly dancer."

"Yes, all feminine nouns."

"But, Jane, what about the women fighting for liberation? They feel they qualify for higher executive jobs. Don't you go along with the liberation movement?"

"Well, personally I'm happy being here in my nice apartment, with all my stocks, with you—"

"Ran third again."

"I don't feel I'm not liberated. If that's what they want, let them have it. Doesn't it to you?"

"Uh, yes, lib and let lib. But you see, Jane, not all women share your opinion that certain jobs have a sexual connotation."

"Please, I never said that."

"You said a telephone operator means a girl. Right?"

"Well, it does. Suppose you called a big company on the phone, what would you do if a man answered the switchboard?"

"I'd hang up. I always hang up when a man answers."

"See? That's what I mean."

"But I happen to know a woman with four grown children. She felt she wanted more out of life; so she took a postgraduate course and earned a doctorate in philosophy. Now she has a professional identity—Dr. Edith Williams."

"Yes, but I'll bet when her children come to visit they call her Mother. And you can put that in your column."

"And smoke it."

42. A NEW HANGUP

Do you know that you are talking 20 per cent longer on each phone call you make this year than you did last year? That's the opinion of the head of the New York State Public Service Commission. He suggests that is one of the reasons our phone service has become so clogged that we can't even get a dial tone.

He's right. And the basic cause is that secretaries have taken to themselves more investigative powers to protect the security and privacy of their employers than they did last year. All of the secretaries are virtuously impregnable. No offense, ladies.

"Hello, may I speak to Mr. Faddle?"

"Who's calling Mr. Faddle?"

"Mr. Ace."

"Can you spell that?"

"Yes"—(pause).

"Hello."

"Oh, you mean you want me to spell it now? It's A-C-E, I think."

"Where are you from, Mr. Ace?"

"Kansas City."

"Are you calling from Kansas?"

"No, this is a local call. Besides, it's not Kansas. You see, there are two Kansas Citys. One is in Kansas and the other in Missouri. I'm from Kansas City, Missouri."

"Are you visiting New York?"

"Well, I've been visiting here, oh, I'd say, day and night for about thirty-five years. May I speak to Mr. Faddle now?"

"Who are you with, Mr. Ace?"

"Well, nobody right now. Oh, my secretary is here, but I can't disturb her. She's on her coffee break, which consists of a chocolate malted and a gooey piece of Danish. I tell you, signing a typed letter she hands me is like a meal in itself. Would you put Mr. Faddle on, please?"

"What is the nature of your business?"

"Well—just a moment, I'm changing ears. There, is that better?"

"Yes, Sir."

"Where were we—oh yes, the nature of my business. I'm a writer by nature. But most of my time is spent in unnatural phone calls. Is Mr. Faddle in?"

"I am not permitted to give that information until I ask him."

"Well, ask him."

"Oh, I'm sorry. I just saw Mr. Faddle go out to lunch just a moment ago."

"Lunch? That's what I was calling about—to tell him I could make that lunch appointment today."

"Oh yes, I just noticed my notes here—you were supposed to call and let him know if you could make it. But since you didn't call, he went out alone."

"Who didn't call? If you weren't so busy playing FBI and CIA, I could have gone with him."

"Well, would you like to make another lunch appointment? Or are you going back to Kansas City—Missouri, that is?"

"I think I will. I can always take my sister to lunch. It's been nice and long chatting with you, Miss uh—"

"Miss Smith."

"Is that S-M-I-T-H?"

"No, it's S-M-Y-T-H."

"That figures. Good-by—forever, that is."

Of course, you know that is not an entirely true picture. His name is not Faddle. It's Fuddle. And I changed her name to protect the guilty. But doubtless it's the employer who has instructed her to put all phone callers through the rack of inquisition. If he had told his secretary to cool it, "Just get the name of the caller and let me know, and I'll tell you if I'm in," this could loosen phone circuits all over the country.

That's the way it's handled in my office. With one slight deviation, over which I have no control. I've instructed her to ask only the name of the caller, relay it to me, and I'll tell her if I'm in. It works perfectly.

I'm always in. I have to be. You see, she sits in the outer office, a call comes in, and with the mouthpiece inches from her lips she shouts over the partition, "It's a Mr. Faddle. Are you in?"

"Yes, I am. And to everybody in this building."

It's always "a" Mr. Faddle. Or "a" Mr. Nichols. Out of sheer force of habit, the other day, she yelled, "It's a Mrs. Ace. Are you in?"

Of course, there are other ways to get to Mr. Faddle

without clogging the phone. I could write him and make a lunch date. But that would clog the mail. I could drive downtown in my car, but that would clog the air. Or I could picket his secretary and shout obscenities. But that would clog the jails.

The only communication left to us is to hold a lunch thought. That would only clog our minds. Which is a state of apathy fervently sought after by the Establishment.

43. GREEN POWER

The stranger phoned and identified himself. He said he is a lawyer, second on the list of six names on their office door, and he has a daughter in college who has been sending him copies of essays she has written in her creative writing course, and he wants my professional opinion as to their merit, which he hopes I will give him if I will be his guest at lunch at his club.

As he spoke I was looking over my list of a dozen cop-outs that I keep handy for such gala occasions, a list that runs from "going on a trip around the world" to "what number are you calling?" As I was about to choose No. 4 (Hong Kong flu), I heard him say:

"And my daughter and I read your column every week in the *Saturday Review* and we value your opinion highly."

"Is tomorrow too soon?" I asked.

The dining room of his exclusive club turned out to be one of those brown, leathery upholstered jobs, and had diners with faces to match. They all looked like Herbert

Hoover. My host seemed to be acquainted with all the members. As he nodded to various men he gave me a short biography of each.

"You know who that is?" he whispered. "He's the head of one of the biggest oil companies in the world. . . . That man is president of one of the richest brokerage houses on Wall Street. . . . That's the owner of one of the largest shipbuilding companies in the United States."

"Tell me only success stories" is the order of our time. This is a throwback to the days at mother's knee when a child was fascinated by stories of the triumph of good over evil, the handsome hero over the ugly villain: the poor boy who shined shoes to pay the greedy landlord with the mortgage, who is about to evict the boy's mother, when the shoeshine boy returns in time to foil the landlord, having become wealthy enough to buy the landlord's sumptuous home and to evict him.

I listened to my host's success stories in quiet amusement until one man passed and he nodded. I asked who that was. "He's a writer," he said. No biographical superlatives. No "head of the biggest," "president of the richest," or "owner of the largest." How he got into this class of the long green was that it's the fashion these days for every club to have its token minority member.

During the Presidential campaign, all candidates acknowledged that there were other classes besides rich and poor. How often did we hear "Justice for all—rich and poor, black and white, young and old"? And even that grouping seemed to disenfranchise millions of uneasy citizens who were unable to identify with those classes. The in-betweens will have to be reckoned with in the next campaign.

"I believe," the campaigner will say, "in justice for all, the rich and the poor, the blacks and the whites, the young and the old, the haves and the hads, the tall and the short, the middle-aged and the he-doesn't-look-that-olds, the birth controllers and the take-a-chancers, the *Ladies' Home Journals* and the *Looks*, the making-both-ends-meet and the credit-card holders, the long-haired and the girls, the childless and the bachelors, and corn-on-the-cob eaters and the dentured, the pepped and the pooped, the oilmen and the income tax payers." Applause, applause, applause.

While I was eating lunch, my host busied himself pointing out several hundred million dollars worth of other celebrities in the room. I didn't catch their names. He didn't throw any. The status was money flow. Even the salad began to have a mint green flavor. I had ordered oysters. They were a disappointment. I thought in a club like this there would have been at least one pearl.

Oh yes, his daughter's essays. They were unusually amusing. Her rhetoric is impeccable, her language picturesque. Turned on as she is against the Establishment, she thankfully manages a delicately biting satire, leaving only tiny teeth marks. I got the feeling that she was surprised at the illogical logic which emerged from the concentric circles by which she reached her zanily perceptive conclusions. And best of all, her fingers, flying busily over her typewriter keys, never left her heart.

Of course, that was not the report I sent her father. Syntax, to him, would be a misspelled stock on the Big Board. I simply wrote him: "Your daughter bids fair to become the head of a rich magazine, and I predict one day she will be owner and president of the largest publishing house in America. The world will be her oyster. With a pearl in it."

44. A BUSINESS THAT WENT SOUR

These days nobody seems able, or willing, to live within his income. A salary check, minus five or six substantial withholdings, needs a substantial plus to meet the high cost of living it up.

To afford the luxuries, a lot of us are scurrying about to find extra jobs to eke out a few extra dollars which in turn aren't eking out as luxuriously as they used to eke out. Moonlighting has become a way of life.

It's all legal and acceptable, unless he's a man in high public office, and he writes a book, gives a lecture, or even shellacs a hit record. For him moonlighting often leads to investigation and public embarrassment. He could get badly burned.

Moonlighting is old stuff. I can tell it like it was, if you don't mind my turning the clock back to the time when I was eleven, which I woefully admit will take a lot of turning back. Got a minute?

At that age I was a movie buff, always in need of some extra income for the flicks. But my parents had me restrained to one movie a week. They maintained that I was already overentertained, what with my stereoptican slides of Niagara Falls, in 3D and living sepia.

Ruminating on how to augment a starvation allowance, it came to me on a hot summer's day to moonlight. I discussed it with three colleagues—two boys and a girl similarly financially embarrassed. We decided to build a lemonade stand.

We envisioned untold wealth. And it would be better left untold, but in the interest of helping a fellow moonlighter, I'll tell it. I can't remember what I had for lunch today, but I have total recall of this misbegotten venture.

Building the stand was easy. An orange crate was our store, and on a tree we hung a crayoned sign that read LEMONADE 1¢ A GLASS. There was a question whether there were two "m's" in lemonade or one. This was quickly and correctly solved when it became obvious the width of our cardboard would not accommodate the extra "m."

The stand finished, things got a little complicated. If you're going to have a sign that says you see lemonade at 1¢ a glass, you darned well better have a bowl of lemonade and glasses. My associates voted three to one that I supply the stuff.

I sneaked into the house and returned with two lemons, a crystal punch bowl, and three of the six matching crystal glasses that my mother treasured as a keepsake from her mother. I was warmly applauded by my co-owners.

Dusk fell quickly in those days, and by the time we were ready to do business, night had fallen. There was not even any moon for this moonlight caper. I got two candles. Another crisis—we needed matches. None of us was permitted to touch matches.

And at this point our first small customer toddled over. She asked for lemonade. I poured it and she drank it down.

"That'll be one cent," I said.

"I haven't got any money," she replied.

"You saw our sign," I remonstrated. "It says one cent."

"I can't read," she replied.

"How'd you know it was lemonade?"

"I can read 'lemonade.'"

I could see she was not going to be our favorite customer.

"Listen," I said, "you don't have to pay for the lemonade if you bring us a match."

She brought us a match. And she must have told every kid in the neighborhood we were giving away free drinks for matches. They came from everywhere.

What can I tell you? On that one bowl of lemonade we took in twenty-six matches. And, oh yes, in that melee the crystal bowl was cracked.

What an investigation that started! What public embarrassment I suffered as my father pronounced: "No more movies for you for the next six weeks"; he meted out "one week for the bowl, one for the lemons, one for the sugar, one for the candles, one for the ice, and one for spelling lemonade with one 'm.'"

"But it *is* only one 'm,'" I argued, suddenly remembering my spelling.

I got a seventh week for arguing.

That's what I've been trying to tell you. No matter

what the rewards, moonlighting is playing with matches. You always wind up getting badly burned.

Although down through the years, as I have sat wearily typing out pieces like this, I've often asked myself, "If my father hadn't put me out of the lemonade business, could I have become the Match King of the world?"

45. THE ARCHITECT

On a corner of Park Avenue in mid-Manhattan there
stood for many years a quaint, four-story, red brick building that housed the American Bible Society. In one of
the windows there was always, on a stand, a king-sized
pulpit Bible, opened to display the quotation of the day.

It was my wont, as I passed every day, to pause for a
moment of brief, but deep, contemplation, to read the
featured passage. The last one I recall reading was "I am
the Lord thy God . . . thou shalt have no other before
me."

Suddenly, the American Bible Society packed its Bible
and its stand and moved out. Then, in 1968, the Republi-
can Party took over the building as its New York campaign headquarters.

Every day I passed, I paused in brief, but deep, contemplation, to read the quotation on the window:
NIXON'S THE ONE.

Later that year, when it turned out Nixon was indeed
the one, the Republicans packed their buttons and their
promises, and moved to Washington, D.C.

Some weeks later, along came the steam shovels, the bulldozers, the dynamite, and the tin-hatted men. Park Avenue, or the Glass Canyon, was to acquire another skyscraper.

This is progress, a more scientific way to reach that heaven which the American Bible Society had for many years been so earnestly selling in its quaint, four-story, red brick building.

The new building is to be thirty-five stories. And yet, from my expertise, gleaned over the years as a sidewalk superintendent, during which I erected at least a dozen of these formidable structures, I have already detected several major mistakes on this new job.

As I pass this project, I pause in brief, but deep, contemplation, through peephole No. 4. The men keep digging, and the steam shovel—well, it don't say nothin', it just keeps shovelin' along. They're so far down now that, from my peephole, the men look like ants. I know our government is making overtures to recognize China, but this is ridiculous.

The pattern never varies. A man blows a whistle, another man sets off a blast of dynamite, and the hungry steam shovel grabs a mouthful of rubble and spews it into the waiting trucks. The trucks go and come up and down a hill of dirt that the steam shovel has left standing.

And that's where they are going to run into their first knotty problem. Once that hill is removed, how, if you don't mind my pointing, will that monster of a steam shovel get out of that hole into which it has painted itself? And how am I going to get out of that lousy metaphor I dug myself into?

The answer is that neither of us will. Yesterday, when

I went to my surveying office at No. 4, the dirt hill road was gone, and the steam shovel was quietly sitting down there getting a tan in the noonday sun.

It was surrounded by a group of the tin-hatted men who were holding a crash luncheon-business conference. I couldn't hear what they were saying between their sandwich bites, but, from the way they gulped their food, it was obvious the topic was "how do we get this damn thing out of here?"

That evening, I passed again when the men were knocking off work. The steam shovel was still down there, but the men were so jolly and carefree that I immediately suspected what they had decided. But they are not going to get away with it.

When that building is up, I will go directly to the sub-subbasement and look for a mound of cement that has the outline of a steam shovel. So when you read that a new thirty-five-story building had to be torn down and put up again, you'll know why.

I know what you're asking. "If you're such an expert, why didn't you warn these workers?" I'll tell you why. When I started superintending construction many years ago—it was the Schenley Building—I detected such a stupid miscalculation through my peephole that I was sure those tin hats had been supplied with the Schenley product.

What a faux pas! They had forgotten to leave space for elevators! Naïve apprentice that I was, I mentioned it to one of the journeymen. He stared, shook his head, walked away. But don't think he didn't hear me. They made space, and to this day there have been elevators there. And not a word of thanks, or even a jigger of the product.

The American Bible Society would have been more charitable. The quotation in the window that day would have read: "Wherefore by their fruits ye shall know them."

46. THE LION AND THE LAMBS

When I was a young man courting a girl, I was ten. She
was eleven. I had an affinity for older women.

We attended the same school in a Midwestern town.
It was my wont, when I saw her walking on the school-
grounds at recess, to attract her attention by turning what
I thought were graceful handsprings. They were handsprings which more often than not found me prostrate
on my aching back. That caused her to giggle, and I was
ecstatic that she had noticed me.

On this schoolground there constantly strolled the tall,
gaunt figure of Mr. Ridgeway, principal. Mr. Ridgeway
as I now recall was 10 feet, 6 inches tall. His hands
clasped behind his back, the principal surveyed with a
jaundiced eye the behavior of the school's hundred or
so pupils.

Pupils who did not conform to his standard of gentle-
manly behavior were punished on the spot. The punishment consisted of walking the grounds with fingers
holding on to Mr. Ridgeway's coattails for all to see. This
was not only disgrace but capital punishment.

After one of my more grotesque handsprings I looked up from the ground and there was Mr. Ridgeway. And there I was for the next fifteen minutes walking the grounds attached to his coattails and wishing I were dead.

In spite of having been on the rack myself, I still harbor a lingering respect and a vestige of fear for school authority. Traumatic as this childhood experience was, I still find myself unable to empathize with the outlandish behavior of Columbia University students who locked their dean and even their teachers in their offices and classrooms.

Sometimes I waver a little when it comes to teachers. I recall Miss Fisher. While Mr. Ridgeway was Enemy No. 1, Miss Fisher was definitely No. 2. Miss Fisher was a stickler for perfection. When she sent me to the blackboard to multiply 46 x 57 (I remember the numbers distinctly) and I came up with the answer of 2,604, Miss Fisher took over and proved that the answer was 2,622.

To have even come up with the 2,600 seemed to me Herculean enough. But not for Miss Fisher. "When you multiplied the 7 x 6, you put down the 4," she said, "and you carried the 2, instead of putting down the 2 and carrying the 4."

I said something the equivalent of "Big deal!", which resulted in her asking me to bring my mother the next day to talk to her. This was the other bit of corporal punishment they doled out. My mother came. Instead of protecting her first-born, my mother chickened. You never heard such disgusting "yes"ings, and "of course"ings, and "I promise it won't happen again"ings.

With that ancient history of persecution and teacher-brutality, wouldn't you think I'd be cheering the university students in their dissidence and rebellion against the establishment? Yet, somehow I am repelled by it.

Even at age ten I think I handled *my* fight against the education establishment more reasonably. As each problem with my educators arose I thought it over calmly. I slept on it. And in my dreams I had Miss Fisher walk a plank 46 inches long and 57 inches wide, and drop 2,622 fathoms into the ocean below. As for Mr. Ridgeway, I simply cut off his coattails. It was all quick, neat, and completely satisfying. No newspaper headlines, no TV cameras, no police. No sweat. Except the cold sweat in which I awoke.

But consider the cold, angry sweat of a student at Columbia who, the news story tells us, came across a policeman, a newspaperman, and three middle-aged men who were standing near one of the university's buildings. In a voice "strangled with fury" he shouted into their faces: "I hope you old . . . die! I hope you old . . . die! Go ahead and watch us and die!"

That's pretty rough talk, and direct. It is known today by the young set as "communicating." But I still think my dreams were made of sterner stuff.

Of course my school days were all once upon a happier time. A time when the three Rs did not stand for Rioting, Ransacking, and holding a teacher for Ransom. That was in the dim past when the song went "School days, school days, dear old golden rule days." When "reading and 'riting and 'rithmetic (were) taught to the tune of a hickory stick." The hickory stick seems to have changed hands. As for the golden rule—we all know what has happened to gold. Dross.

47. WHAT EVER HAPPENED TO FIDO?

As a writer, I am often called upon by friends to lend my
superb talent to naming their dogs. They've come to the
right place. I've gained some renown in this field, even
if I do say so myself, because we once had a West High-
land terrier, whose fur, you know, is pure white. I named
him Blackie. This was always good for a big laugh and
some applause for my ingenuity.

This rare gift of naming dogs is second nature to me.
And I am happy to oblige many friends who call to take
advantage of it. Dog names come to me in a flash of in-
spiration. As one came when a friend called to announce
she had acquired a little French poodle.

"What do you think of the name 'Mignon'?" she asked.

"No good," I replied quickly. "Too many French
poodles are named 'Mignon'! I suggest you call her
'Filet.'"

"Oh," she said, "there's someone at the door. I'll call
you back."

She never did. But I'm sure she loved it, and little Filet
has found herself a friendly home.

I've had only one rejection. A family of relatives in the Midwest wrote that their children wanted a dog. The pet of their choice was a sheep dog, a little pup who would grow up one day to eat them out of house and bone. With my usual flash, I wrote suggesting their sheep dog should be called "Baldy."

That was almost a year ago. Recently, I stopped off to visit them and was met at the door by a huge carpet of white and gray fur that hurled itself at me and licked my glasses.

"Hello, Baldy," I said. "Glad to see me, aren't you, Baldy? OK, Baldy, that's enough. Sit, Baldy."

He sat. And one of the children said, "Gee, he sat. He never does that for us."

"He doesn't do anything when we command him," said the mother.

"Besides," said the smallest of the tots, "his name ain't Baldy. It's Oliver."

Although I can't take rejection, I put on my best smile and said, "Well, hello, Oliver. Shake hands, Oliver."

Oliver stared at me and backed up. Like a flash, I realized the problem. He didn't like the name of Oliver. Dog lovers don't know it, but dogs are sensitive about their names. Take the case of another dog I know that was originally named Rover.

Rover was a ferocious-looking bulldog, which the children of the family had named Rover, because, as one of the youngsters told me, "he roved into our back yard." Rover was of mixed breed, obviously came from disadvantaged parents, had little education, and was not interested in finding a place for himself in the mainstream.

They had sent Rover to a school for dogs to learn to

heel and sit. But to no avail. Rover soon became a drop-out, and returned home listless and apathetic, still refusing to conform, or to obey any command.

The parents had hoped he would be a fun companion for the kids and also be a watchdog. But Rover showed no signs of belligerence. He was so lackadaisical he had never even barked. A member of the Silent Majority.

The children tried to teach him to bark. "Arf, arf," they shouted at Rover. Rover rejected "Arf" as any kind of hot rhetoric suitable to our times. Actually, only one dog I ever heard of said "Arf." That was Sandy, Orphan Annie's shaggy friend.

I came into the picture when the father told me about the trouble the family was having with Rover.

"Rover?" I said. "That's no name for a bulldog. I suggest you rename him 'Peace.' You'll thank me someday."

He phoned two days later.

"Man," he shouted, "did you get me into a peck of trouble! I have two summonses here, from the postman, and the milkman. Peace not only barked at them, but he bit 'em."

"Of course," I said. "It's the uniform. The symbol of war. He's trying to protect you from the enemy at your door."

"But he's expanded the war. Today, Peace bit 'em at our neighbor's door."

"Naturally. He's not going to let the enemy find sanctuary in your neighbor's territory," I replied.

"Yeh? Well, not only did he bite them, but Peace tore into the cat next door, and they had to take it to a hospital, and our neighbors are calling the ASPCA to take our dog away. What do I do?"

"Negotiate," I advised quickly. "It's the only way you can keep Peace."

Perhaps you miss the point of that subtle allegory. If it's too obscure for you, it can be best explained in a moral —without which no allegory should be.

MORAL: If you're going to write a column about naming dogs, don't let the subject slip too far away, else you wind up with a moral that cats and dogs fight like people.

48. ADVICE TO THE LAUGHLORN

I asked the average, attractive, young lady, who is shopping for a husband, what she expects her man-to-be to be.

"Well," she said, "first and most important of all, he must have a good sense of humor." Or to quote her more directly, "A good sensa humor."

"That's a good start," I conceded. "But tell me, average, young, attractive lady, what are the other qualifications you fondly seek?"

"I fondly seek," she replied, "a man who will be compatible, gentle, compassionate, chivalrous, magnanimous, thoughtful, considerate, kindly, and well off."

I tried to plumb the depth of each of these high expectations, but she side-stepped the plumbing, and said only, "He will understand what I mean after we're married."

However, I did manage to fathom her definitions of all these prerequisites:

Compatible: easy to mold.

Gentle: to her mother.

Compassionate: no children for three years.

Chivalrous: he must say "Good morning" to the house-maid and to the cook she plans to hire.

Magnanimous: separate credit cards.

Thoughtful: call from his office hourly.

Considerate: never bring unexpected guests to dinner.

Kindly: see *magnanimous, thoughtful,* and *considerate.*

Well off: he is, but he doesn't know it.

All these unspoken "understandings" can get a guy into a heap of trouble. (See North Vietnam.) Unless he has a good sense of humor.

Which brings us to the interesting, albeit unimportant, question: What is a "good" sense of humor? Difficult to define, because humor comes in several levels. What is humorous to one man may be a pain in the neck to an-other. Or what is humorous to one man may be humorism to another.

What people will laugh at has been a prevailing ques-tion in the mass media for many years. Having supplied humor to the comedians of radio and television since "Why does a chicken cross the street?" was a *pièce de résistance,* I have heard thousands of funnymen question the value of thousands of funny lines.

"I understand the joke," they say, "but will they laugh at it in Oshkosh?"

"Have you ever been to Oshkosh?" I always inquired.

"Well, no, but—"

"Why don't you pack your Oshkosh bag and go there? You'll discover they're not stupid at all."

Incidentally, Oshkosh was not the only town so hon-ored. They have also said a certain joke would not be understood in Podunk, Wichita, Bayonne, and Tulsa.

I tried several times to get one such bit of humor on

the idiot cards for several funnymen to read. They said it would not be understood in any of the above-mentioned towns.

This is the ill-fated joke:

"I see they're putting a clock on the Leaning Tower of Pisa in Italy."

"Why," asks the straight man, "are they putting a clock on the Leaning Tower of Pisa in Italy?"

"Because the Italians feel what's the use of having the inclination if you don't have the time."

None of them gave an intelligible reason for turning it down. But one young comedian gave me an inkling when he mumbled something about "Inclination—it's too big a word—they won't get it." Subsequently, I have used the joke on the lecture circuit and can report they "got it" in towns from New Hampshire to California.

But laughing together at the same joke is not what our young lady on the prowl for a husband with a good sense of humor has in mind. She's projecting a life of wedded bliss with a fellow who will join her in laughing off burnt dinners, bent fenders, and some myth math on the stubs of their joint checking account.

However, this joint laughter through the semi-serious, semi-comic incidentals of everyday life takes time, years, a heap of living together. There is an old fishwife's tale— and I believe in old fishwives, even though they haven't been mentioned in the Lib movement—that man and wife, living together through thirty or forty years of marriage, gradually begin to think alike, to laugh alike, and even to look alike. Except for the hair curlers in the mornings.

So, if our young lady continues looking for a young man at the ready with a risibility tailor-made to hers, she's on the road to a lot of short, broken engagements, and will be kept pretty busy returning engagement rings and shower gifts.

TV

Shorthand for Trivia

49. THE UNCOMMON COLD

The Federal Trade Commission is casting a jaundiced eye on "deceptive commercials" on TV. And high time.

This winter our set has been saturated to overflowing with nose sprays, throat gargles, cough syrups, fizzing stomach-settlers, breath-sweetening lotions, and gallons of anti-freeze. It gets very sloshy around our set.

The FTC maintains that while anti-freeze does the job it advertises, there is a possibility of its damaging the cooling system. The FTC wants the anti-freeze manufacturers to include in their commercials: CAUTION—ANTI-FREEZE MAY BE HAZARDOUS TO YOUR COOLING SYSTEM.

But I have my own favorite deceptive commercial, to which I now call your attention. A sickly, forlorn-looking little guy in a bathrobe whines pathetically to his wife: "I feel terrible. I've been coughing, my throat is scratchy, and I could use a little rest."

His tender helpmate pours a shot glass of some green stuff and says, "Here, drink this." He gulps it and says, "You're a good wife." And she says, "I know." It tears at your heart.

But sentiment aside, it seems to me that the green stuff

hasn't been doing the job it advertises. For three months this winter, he's been swigging it, and every time I look in on him he seems to be failing. But she keeps pouring, and he keeps drinking, and he says, "You're a good wife," and she says, "I know."

This business of coughing and scratching has been hanging on too long. I think what he needs is another opinion. I've even watched *The Interns* to see if he showed up on one of their critical lists. Not there. But night after night, week after week, she pours—he drinks —"You're a good wife"—"I know."

I'm beginning to suspect the reason she won't have a doctor in is that it's only when he's feeling sick and she nurses him that she ever hears him admit, "You're a good wife."

I got so uptight, I even called the network to inquire about his condition, and ask why they didn't call in Marcus Welby, M. D., for consultation. The girl was rather hostile, but finally told me that the young man was a fine actor who was simulating sickness, is in good health, and collecting checks every week for his simulated malaise.

I was relieved. Then it struck me that if he was really only simulating sickness, he didn't need the advertised medicine he was drinking. Therefore, that green stuff also had to be simulated. Now what could that be? Of course! She had been pouring, and he had been guzzling crème de menthe! Now there's something that can really blow your cooling system.

While we're on the deceptive commercial kick, I wonder if the FTC watched the ABC network a Sunday or three ago. All that week they had been running house commercials advertising the forthcoming film *The King and I*. Since that classic Rodgers and Hammerstein musical has always been a favorite of mine, I made a point to see it.

That was a deceptive commercial. Because, came that Sunday evening, what we saw, from 5 to 8 o'clock, was a slew of commercials, in between which were scenes from *The King and I*.

For three hours, 180 minutes, the film was interrupted every ten minutes for herds of long and loud-sell sales pitches, plus several "house" commercials showing interminably long scenes from next week's old movies.

These interruptions ran about four minutes each and seemed longer. Figure it out for yourself. Every ten minutes for 180 minutes, comes to eighteen interruptions. And at four minutes each, it comes to seventy-two minutes. For more than an hour out of the three hours, this lovely movie was chopped to pieces. Too high a price for any movie.

Once upon a happier time, a simple station break meant a few seconds time out to announce "This is ABC, the American Broadcasting Company." Now even the station breaks are deceptive. The time out now includes information on what to do if you suffer from sink stains, psoriasis, dull floors, bad breath, diaper rash, cavities, killing girdles, falling cakes. I've even begun not to like Sara Lee.

Always mindful of our health, they also prescribe medicines we should take to relieve indigestion, insomnia, irregularity, acidity, gastritis, headaches, arthritis, and for tired blood, "the nicest thing a girl can do for herself."

If we swallow all that, we are destined to become victims of pre-medicated murder.

50. THOSE BLIP BLIP CENSORS
BLIP THE HELL OUT OF TV

CEN'SOR, n. (L., SCISSORS). *A man walking at night on a street sees a light in the window and says, "A mother praying for the safe return of her boy." A second man sees the light and says, "Oh boy, hanky-panky going on up there." That second man is a censor.*

There have been a lot of exciting happenings in TV these last few weeks. Not on the home screens, heaven forbid, but in the offices of the network executives and in Congress.

At the moment, the main issue is whether TV programs should be censored by the Government, by the networks, or by Senator Pastore. This was dramatized by the sudden cancellation by the CBS network of one of its better and more meaningful programs. The argument against censorship is basic: Today the Smothers Brothers, tomorrow the Lennon Sisters.

Censorship, if allowed to prevail, could easily spread across the TV schedules to any Tom, Dick, or *Laugh-In.*

In spite of the fact that brother Tom is constantly quoted as saying that nobody is censoring *Laugh-In*, so why pick on his program? This could only lead to Congress's censoring *Laugh-In*.

The two programs, however, are disparately motivated. The Smothers, in their revolt against our times, present their unhappiness with the Establishment as a crusade— always partisan. Dan Rowan and Dick Martin in a cascade of humor throw one-liners indiscriminately at all sacred cows.

This is in the tradition of Will Rogers. When he said, "We have the best Congress money can buy," he didn't specify names or point satirically at Democrats or Republicans. Nor does Bob Hope in his masterful monologues seem intent on embarrassing either party or any particular man in high office. He scatters his targets and the darts land where they may.

Censorship is not new in the mass media. Years ago, Fred Allen, a gentleman and a writer-performer of impeccable taste, was in the vanguard of the avant-garde. Every week he was locked in struggle with a bluenosed censor with pencil to match. But Mr. Allen solved his problems quietly, without incurring the wrath of the network.

Each week he would deliberately insert in his scripts three obviously unacceptable quips that were considered in that day "excessive permissiveness." In the final settlement with the censor, he would offer to take out those three if the censor would permit the rest of the script to stand. This compromise always worked, calmly, and without public pronouncement by Mr. Allen to impair the image of the network. Which is being bruited about in

TV circles as the reason behind the reason for the cancellation of the exacerbated and loquacious Smothers.

Also there are those cynics who wonder if it was truly a dirty word that caused the Smothers Brothers cancellation. They say it was a dirty number. The number is twenty-four. Which is where the brothers had dropped in the Nielsen standings.

The Smothers quarrel began a month or two ago when CBS would not permit their show to go on the air, because it hadn't been presented in time for the network censors to examine the script for "excessive permissiveness." So the program was held up while the censors did their blipping in two particular segments.

One was a line in a routine by a guest comedian on the show. (Blip, blip, blip.) The other was a line used by Joan Baez in introducing one of her folk songs. She had explained in the original script that the song was part of an album she had recently recorded, and was dedicated to her husband, David, who was being sent to prison in June because he was not too enthusiastic about going to Vietnam. As a matter of fact, he had refused to be drafted. In the show as finally aired, the line spoken was "dedicated to my husband, David, who is going to prison in June." (Blip, blip, blip.)

However, the censors, in their zeal to blip the comedian and Miss Baez, either overlooked a questionable joke by the Smothers, or they didn't quite get it, but which was "excessive permissiveness." I'm an ardent fan of the brothers, and I am as liberated in my rhetoric as the next girl, but in this family magazine I wouldn't repeat the eight-letter word. (That'll keep you Double-Crostic fans busy.)

The bad, bad word was not actually spoken on the show. It was implied by a clean sound-alike, seven-letter word which was spoken by Dick Smothers and reacted to by his brother Tom. If your curiosity is piqued, I'll spell it out.

The brothers were singing an exciting, guitar accompanied arrangement of the Volga Boatman song. Tom was so carried away that he stopped midway in the song, to describe the scene that ensued when the men arrived and were welcomed by the peasants on shore.

"They were so happy," he said, (and I paraphrase it) "that the boatmen and the peasants improvised a frenetic Russian dance. A huge sort of ballet—you know, a ballet like up—"

"Bolshoi," Dick offered.

"No, honest they did," said Tom.

51. HOW TO SUCCEED IN NOT GETTING
AN AWARD WITHOUT TRYING

I know I promised the other day when I put down the
Emmy awards as an exercise in futility that I would not
devote any more space to TV until next season. But since
the column appeared, I have heard a rumble of mutter-
ings suggesting that I was crying in my glass of the juice
of the grape before it had reached fermentation, because
I never got an award.

That is your right, in accord with Article 1 of the
Amendments to the Constitution, which states that the
Congress shall make no law abridging the freedom of
mutter. A man's best friend is, let us always remember,
his mutter.

But you are wrong. Getting awards is an everyday happening around here. They are presented to me when the
mailman makes his rounds. Even this morning he came
in and stood before me with a letter in his hand. Having
lately watched so many of the award presentations on
TV, I automatically rose to the occasion.

"The envelope, please," I said.

He handed it over, and I read aloud: "Dear Sir: I enjoy your column in *Saturday Review*. It is always the first thing I read in the magazine."

The mailman applauded and shook my hand. It's a daily occurrence. Of course, it's not like getting an award on a TV show glittering with stars. But what it lacks in pomp, it makes up in circumspection.

A lot of those first-thing-I-read-in-the-magazine letters come in. They are my Oscars, my Tonys, my Emmys. Also my Pulitzers, my Peabodys, my Nobels. And it doesn't bother me one bit when quite often letters misdirected to my desk and opened by mistake say the first thing they read is Cleveland Amory, John Ciardi, or Henry Hewes. Each to his own circumspection, I always say.

I'm happy the way I get my awards, despite the mailman who, when I read the letters to him, always says, "Shoulda got that award on TV." I doubt I shoulda. Also I doubt the networks woulda. So we're even there.

No self-respecting network would schedule an award show that runs less than two-and-a-half hours. A program just to give me an award would run not more than ten minutes, including six commercials. And since I'm the only nominee, I wouldn't have to sit there until they handed an Emmy to the nut who mixes the best psychedelic colors, and to the madman who makes the loudest thunder and lightning. Also, by eliminating nervous Don Knotts we would save at least a half-hour.

Of course, a network would insist on Goldie Hawn to open the envelope if she's available. If she isn't, I would take Lilli Palmer. Even if Goldie Hawn *is* available, I would take Lilli Palmer. And to accept the award for me, I would prefer Frances Dee.

Oh, I didn't tell you. I wouldn't be there. It would be

my luck to make television history, sitting there dressed
to my nines (wherever they are, R. L. Stevenson never
told), the only nominee, and then not go get the award.
That would be a rejection my psychiatrist could never
rationalize.

This is a pattern I have easily and scrupulously ad-
hered to in all my years of writing—not to get an award
publicly. No, scratch that. Some years ago the National
Academy of Arts and Sciences did nominate me for an
Emmy for having written the *Perry Como Show*.

I was prepared with a vial of glycerin to simulate tears
and an acceptance speech thanking American Airlines
for getting me to the Coast.

All to no avail. I was nosed out by *Gilligan's Island*.
Just as in the category for best actor on the Oscar TV
show, Richard Burton was nosed out by John Wayne.
And that is not immodestly to consider myself the Richard Burton of writers. But at the very least I think I could
have shown up in a photo-finish dead heat with *Gilligan's
Island*.

Mr. Wayne in his acceptance speech graciously conceded, if he had known that all it took to win an Oscar
was the eye-patch he wore in his latest picture, he would
have worn an eye-patch years ago. Today John Wayne,
tomorrow Moshe Dayan!

No, I'm content to receive my awards in anonymity
before an audience of one mailman. Don't I miss the spotlight? Not at all. A spotlight is an ephemeral thing. Today magenta, tomorrow blackout. Besides, too bright a
spotlight fades my suit.

But that's show business. As Irving Berlin put it,
"There's no business like show business." Everything
about it is appalling.

52. THERE'S GOLD IN THEM THERE PILLS

Actors who appear in most TV commercials have a good thing going for them. They are paid $120 for making the first sixty-second film, and they keep receiving money every time the commercial appears after the first run. This is lovingly known to commercial actors as "residuals."

This is for actors who take medicine, shampoo their hair, or drink beer. However, cigarette advertising is something else. If an actor appears on a commercial for the American Cancer Society, he is washed up as a smoker on a commercial produced by a tobacco company.

Mr. Richard J. Lord, president of Lord, Geller, Federico and Partners, Inc., puts it this way: "If a guy appears in an anti-smoking film, and then two weeks later is seen in a commercial smoking a Salem cigarette, it's going to look very strange."

Not only is it going to look strange, but the pay is strange. The actor who speaks out against cigarettes receives the regular fee of $120. There is no residual in cancer. One actor who turned down the ACS offer said: "If there had been residuals from anti-smoking films, I would have done it."

It seemed to this observer that a non-smoking actor is more deserving of a residual, figuring his lifespan and all that.

Close to $1 billion is spent annually producing and presenting TV commercials. An actor can make as much as $10,000 a year for only a one-minute spot of acting. And the advertising writers who conceive these commercials get astronomical salaries.

All these high numbers appealed to my natural greed and cupidity. One day, while lunching with a man who operates a TV production company, I wondered aloud if I could get in on this bonanza.

"Have you ever written any commercials before?" he asked.

"No," I replied, "but for all that money I'm willing to prostitute my art and become a gentleman of the evening."

He said OK. And he mentioned a product for which he was seeking a commercial. It wasn't a cigarette, so I had a go at it. You know, all those residuals.

In a few minutes I wrote my first television scenario for a one-minute commercial. In leaving it to your judgment I won't divulge the name of the product until after you've read this:

SCENE ONE . . . MUSIC SOFTLY UNDER

A LITTLE GIRL'S PLAYROOM. SHE STANDS BESIDE A LARGE DOLL HOUSE WITH TWO DOLLS IN HER ARMS. AS SHE PLACES ONE OF THE DOLLS ON ONE BED SHE SAYS:
GIRL: Time for bed now.

SHE PLACES THE SECOND DOLL ON THE OTHER BED AND
SPEAKS.

GIRL: Go to sleep, baby.

THE NARRATOR THEN SPEAKS OFF CAMERA.

NARRATOR: The things you treasure should be beautifully
housed.

SCENE TWO

A BACKYARD WITH A SMALL BOY SITTING ON THE GRASS BE-
SIDE A DOGHOUSE. HE HAS TWO SMALL PUPPIES. HE LIFTS ONE
AND CAREFULLY PUTS IT INTO THE DOGHOUSE. HE SPEAKS
SOFTLY.

BOY: Go into your house.

THEN HE PUTS THE OTHER PUP IN AS HE SAYS:

BOY: Time to rest now.

NARRATOR SPEAKS AGAIN OFF CAMERA.

NARRATOR: Prized possessions should be comfortably
housed.

SCENE THREE

A BIRD'S NEST IN A TREETOP . . . TWO BIRDS ARE IN IT. WE
HEAR THE SOUND OF TWO BIRDS CHIRPING. THE NARRATOR
SPEAKS AGAIN OFF CAMERA.

NARRATOR: Adorable things should be comfortably nested.

SCENE FOUR

A MONTAGE OF ALL THREE SCENES. THE LITTLE GIRL PULLING
COVER OVER THE DOLLS. . . . THE LITTLE BOY PUSHING ONE
PUPPY BACK INTO THE DOGHOUSE. . . . THE BIRDS IN THE

TREETOP, CHIRPING. OVER THIS MONTAGE, THERE IS SUPER-
IMPOSED, IN A LONG SHOT, THE PRODUCT WHICH IS BEING AD-
VERTISED . . . IT COMES SLOWLY FORWARD UNTIL IT IS IN
CLOSE-UP. UNDER THE CLOSE-UP THERE APPEARS THE BRAND
NAME OF THE BRA.

P.S.: What can I tell you? They turned it down. Said it
wasn't funny enough.

53. TV CAN BE TERRIBLY VEXING

How to Talk Back to Your Television Set is the title of a new book published by Atlantic-Little, Brown, and written by Nicholas Johnson, your friendly neighborhood Federal Communications Commissioner.

It's a book you should have at hand to read every time you get mad at your TV set, which should put it high on the list of the Ten Most Often Read Books.

Mr. Johnson addresses himself to every viewer whose sensitivities are offended by what TV offers as entertainment, and tells you how you can go about improving it.

"Shouting exhortations at an edifice is a poor substitute for some structural changes," he says. So he has included some pages of names and addresses to which you can write.

As a member of long standing of the People's Communications Commission, a new and just-this-minute-formed organization, I have written as many cleverly satiric letters to the networks as any viewer, and I have come to the sad conclusion that they consider my handiwork the product of a deranged mind. If you look in the files of the networks' incoming mail, you will find me listed under C, for crackpot.

One campaign I waged was for a simple little grammatical error that seems to have infiltrated the air waves, especially on the talk shows:

"The people are responding in a way that are not acceptable," said a man the other night. Would it hurt if the host stopped the show and said: "That should be *is* not acceptable." "Is" is the predicate of the singular subject, "way." A little knowledge for the viewers is not all that dangerous.

A lawyer said: "I've advised my client not to testify till we know what the nature of the charges are."

The announcer of a golf tournament: "The car carrying the players have just arrived at the fifteenth hole."

Senator John C. Stennis (Miss.): "We will have to pass a Constitutional amendment to say that under certain facts a person would forfeit their right to a trial."

This laissez-faire attitude toward the English language does not enhance TV's charm. It's as if the networks have broken out in a massive epidemic of pluralcy.

Fortunately, all TV is not like that. There is still a half-hour oasis on NBC Monday nights in a program called *My World and Welcome to It*. Literate, expertly written, acted, directed, and produced, the program is delightfully unlike the year-in-and-out, factory-made domestic situation comedies that clutter our sets. It is pure James Thurber.

So naturally NBC has announced that *My World* will be dropped next season. But the network has a good reason, other than the fact that the show didn't get an acceptable rating. The three networks, we are told, are concentrating on programs that have "relevance and social awareness." So in place of *My World*, NBC will give us a half-hour Red Skelton show, marked down from the hour he had on CBS, which canceled him after nineteen years.

My World was highly recommended (G) in this space some time ago. The mail response was from viewers who had been watching it, and thank-you notes from those who hadn't. Nicholas Johnson, of course, would have been happier if they had written the network. Many of the writers had a valid reason: "Whenever I've written a network to praise a program, it inevitably was taken off the next season. I don't want to jinx this one." And now, as my wife is wont to say, "the chickens have come home to roast."

Mrs. Bettye K. Hoffmann, in charge of TV mail at NBC, recently admitted there had been a lot of warm letters about *My World* from the "better educated, teachers, ministers." There had also been some from people who objected to what they claimed was misogyny—the men in the show hated their wives and all women.

Not true. Those who were favored to have met James Thurber knew him as a gentle man. His battle between the sexes was all skirmish, no search and destroy.

There were also letters, Mrs. Hoffmann says, from orthodontists who embraced the extraoral anchorage worn over her teeth and from ear to ear by the adorable little girl in *My World*. It was a selling point to convince their frightened little patients who doubtlessly thought of it as another form of misogyny.

Postscript: Mr. Mort Werner, head of NBC programing, when asked earlier this season which program he was most proud of, said *My World and Welcome to It*.

That's the pride that goeth before a fall season.

54. SIMON SAYS

For some time now I have been basking, though modestly, in the glow of being a celebrity. And it's not because of any special phosphorescence I give off personally. It's due to the fact that playwright Neil Simon, in interviews on TV talk shows, has mentioned that he broke into comedy writing twenty-three years ago as a member of my staff of radio writers.

In case you've been out of the country the past nine years, visiting your money in Switzerland, let it be retold that Neil Simon is the author of nine successive hit Broadway plays, beginning with *Come Blow Your Horn* and on through *The Odd Couple, Plaza Suite, Promises, Promises,* and other titles I should remember but don't. I've been so busy being a proxy celebrity.

It all began several years ago when, on the day after one of Mr. Simon's hits had opened, someone phoned to ask me if I had watched last night's Johnny Carson TV show. I replied I hadn't, because if I'm up that late I'm usually asleep.

"Well," said this friend, "you sure missed it. Neil Simon told Carson that he got his start as a comedy writer on your staff."

I was quite pleased. I preened a little. I said it was true. But I didn't tell him that my total recall of the faces of that staff of eight neophyte writers was nil.

I did remember the names of two talented brothers, Neil and Danny Simon, who were included in the group I had hired at CBS to train to raise the level of radio comedy. But I thanked him for calling to tell me.

"Hey," phoned another friend, "I didn't know you started Neil Simon as a comedy writer. He told it last night on the Carson show." There were more calls, and soon I was saying, "Yes, I always predicted he would be a successful playwright and turn out nine hits in a row."

By day's end, Neil Simon began zooming more clearly into the delayed replay of my polluted nostalgia.

It all comes back—we wrote in conference. That is, I would sit at the typewriter, and my staff would throw jokes at me. We would discuss their worth, and use those I felt would work.

I remember mostly that Neil Simon was a shy and quiet-spoken young fellow. He volunteered very few lines. It was his brother Danny who hollered out the funnier bits. I didn't know until a year after we broke up that Neil had whispered most of the gags to Danny, who tossed them into the pot.

The scripts we wrote were used in an hour radio program that CBS had given us as a laboratory, a hodge-podge of jokes to be hosted by Robert Q. Lewis. Neil Simon was later to say in a newspaper interview that he hated writing for this and, more important, radio shows to which he graduated.

He also said in a recent interview that he is not going to write any more plays just for laughs. There would be something "meaningful," he said, a message of some sort, a pause in the laughter for a tough look at our social mores.

In the "golden days of radio," as they say, the young writers never bothered with messages. A joke was a joke was a joke. One or two of the more intrepid writers tried to sneak in a daring message such as "Honesty is the best policy." Or "Early to bed and early to rise," or a whopper like "Do unto others as you would have them do unto you."

But never, never did a radio writer dare to fool with something like "Thou shalt not covet thy neighbor's wife." As a matter of fact, they don't fool with that message now either. Coveting is out. In today's entertainment, movies especially, nobody "covets" a neighbor's wife. He just takes.

Which is the theme of the third act of Simon's latest comedy hit, *Last of the Red Hot Lovers.* After the play opened and the critics had spent superlative adjectives as if they were credit cards, Neil Simon went on another talk show and again mentioned our early association.

More phone calls. And I got that old celebrity feeling again. This was my ninth time around as a celebrity, and I should have been able to handle it more gracefully.

But as the telephoners grew more expansive in their accreditations ("That Neil Simon's sure lucky you let him work with you"), my responses grew apace. I added lines such as "Yes, looks like we've written another hit."

But it was at the Friars for lunch that day that I went completely ape. I was greeted too cordially by brother Friars, who recognize a celebrity when they see one. An hour later when the waiter placed my check before me, I signed it: "To Harry, with love, 50-cent tip."

55. BE MY GUEST

If you're wondering why your favorite TV programs are
to disappear from your sets next season, you can blame
it on the two eye-counting outfits that make these reports: the Audience Research Bureau and the A. C.
Nielsen Company.

How they accomplish this arithmetical feat has been a
trade secret all these years. Fortunately for you, I've unearthed it. The latest ARB count reveals there is a "wide-
spread, unaccountable, and unbelievable decline" in TV
viewers. The Nielsen people say there is a decline, but
it's only minor and isolated.

What it amounts to is ARB counts each eye glued to
the set and multiplies by two. Nielsen multiplies by four.
In any case, there is a decline. And high time.

One reason for viewers' disenchantment is the monoto-
nous repetition of celebrity guests who appear on the
programs of celebrity hosts. This is especially true re-
garding TV specials.

Most often these celebrities who are guests don't appear for money. It's what is called an exchange. "You
guest on my show, and I'll guest on yours." One ham
washes the other.

For instance, when you see the celebrated Bob Hope show up on a celebrated *Bing Crosby Special,* you can safely bet two cans of Minute Maid to one that Crosby will show up on the next *Bob Hope Special.*

Similarly, Hope was recently a guest on the *Perry Como Special.* And who do you think showed up as a celebrity guest on the next *Bob Hope Special?* Not Phil Brito!

Carol Burnett does it, Jim Nabors does it, Lucille Ball does it, Tom Jones does it, even the Lennon Sisters, and the birds do it. All fall in line. This overexposure may make celebrities household words. But not household pets. For heaven's sake, even Vice President Agnew has cut down on his TV appearances.

Oh, I see a lady has raised her hand. Yes, Madame, what is it? A very good question: "What is a TV celebrity?"

Well, celebrities come in two categories—the "Now" celebrity and the "Then" celebrity. Follow closely:

A Now celebrity is a young man, wearing a guitar, who has just come from Nashville, where the action is, with his recordings of folk, rock, and country songs.

A Then celebrity is an older man, wearing a money belt over his girdle, who has just come from the bank with a recording of the money he made in the early days of TV, where the action once was.

The name of the game is a high ARB or Nielsen TV rating. A Then celebrity can usually be depended on to get a big rating, but to play it safe he hires a Now celebrity, hoping to attract the young viewers.

A celebrity ceases to be a celebrity when his rating drops. Jackie Gleason, for instance. The Great One has always rated high doing *The Honeymooners.* When he decided to change to variety programs, down went his rating. The network said he could stay on if he would go back to his original format. But no, it was too much work, now that he'd gotten rich and thin.

Perry Como, once a weekly giant in the ratings, could have stayed on, but, when the network started talking ratings and change of format, he retired to a golf course. Now he does one special a year. He still sings like an angel. Obviously, he's decided to save it till he gets up there.

Oh, before I forget, there is another kind of celebrity guest—the Instant Celebrity, who overnight makes the front pages. Instant Celebrities don't last long. They are immediately grabbed off, usually by the alert Ed Sullivan.

I'm thinking of that poor rich lad who recently came of age and inherited millions. What made him a celebrity was his announcements in the papers and on TV that he was giving it all to the needy, on a first come, first served basis.

After Mr. Sullivan gave the boy his usual obscurely eloquent introduction, we were treated to the pathetic sight of a young man who mumbled a poem by Bob Dylan to what could loosely be called his own accompaniment on his guitar. Mr. Sullivan gave him his special "Let's hear it" treatment, the boy bowed and departed, saying he was giving away trillions of dollars.

I don't know how high the Instant Celebrity raised the Sullivan rating that night. But it couldn't have been as high as the papers suggested the kid had been when he announced his giveaway. And so another Instant Celebrity had gone to pot.

God

...is in His Heaven,
and All Is Wrong with the World

56. GOD IS ALIVE AND WELL AND LIVING IN TERROR

And so it came to pass in Heaven that it was the week before Christmas. And the Heavenly Hosts had long been busy preparing to celebrate the glorious Day of His birth.

The fleecy clouds had been decked with boughs of holly. And tinsel hung from all the stars, "blessed candles of the night." From the rehearsal halls were heard the choral voices of Angels, trolling the ancient Yuletide carols.

The Streets of Solid Gold were paved over with banks of fake snow. And in a place of honor stood last year's little Christmas tree, which shone like new, resplendently trimmed with globes of imitation crystal in living color.

And so it was when St. Peter stood at his Gate, humming "Silent Night" as he dusted an old wreath of holly to hang over his pearly portal, there came to him a messenger with a memo.

It was marked URGENT and it read: "Due to the violent hatred and divisiveness on one of our planets, this year's Birthday celebration is canceled. Stop all preparations." Signed, "G."

The venerable Keeper of the Gate recognized Wrath when he saw it. That the turmoil on one tiny speck in the vast firmament of His Kingdom should deprive them of this Joyous Day of celebration was beyond his comprehension. He was astonished.

A voice came thundering through the intercom: "I am not interested in your comprehension! You are only astonished, I am terrified. Until the cause of these unprecedented hatreds is discovered, and Order restored under Justice, there will be no more Birthday celebrations. And tell those Angels to stop that singing!"

And suddenly the Heavens were stilled. In moments the Angels came scurrying to the Gate. St. Peter told them of conditions on Earth. Their disappointment was apparent. They babbled in chorus, protesting their displeasure.

He stood helplessly among them. The Word has been spoken. There was no appeal. Unless . . . unless conditions down there could, by some miracle, be transformed into Peace and Goodwill. Some small miracle, one in St. Peter's province. He called for quiet.

"There is one chance," St. Peter told them. "We have a full week. Theresa," he said pointing to one of the more voluble dissenting Angels, "you will fly down to Earth and discover the cause of these violent hatreds. You will report to me as soon as you have, if you'll pardon the pun, unearthed the cause. Remember, time is of the essence."

And so it was that Theresa flew down and landed, unplanned, on Broadway and 44th Street, attracted by the lights of The Great White Way. That very night she called St. Peter on the Celestial phone.

"St. Peter, this is Theresa. I have discovered the source

of these hatreds. It's a place called Broadway. The people are drawn here like moths to the flame, to watch other people whose faces are painted and who gather in a place called Sardi's—a restaurant—where they speak sweetly to each other while stabbing each other in the back. I'm frightened. May I come back, please?"

St. Peter scoffed. This was merely acceptable human behavior. He ordered Theresa to investigate further and to discover the cause of this terrestrial upheaval.

He didn't hear from her for three days. Then the phone rang again. It was the Angel Theresa. "Hello, Peter darling, this is Terry! I'm out in Hollywood now! It's terribly groovy, and I've discovered the root of all this evil. It's on a street called The Strip where young men congregate in multitudes. Their hair grown long, their faces filled with beards, they wear sandals and unseemly robes. They are the cause. I am told they are spread across the earth, millions in number. They say they are doing their 'Thing.'"

And St. Peter reported this investigation to Him. "It's the young men with beards and long hair and sandals who have created hatred and divisiveness."

"No, no," replied God. "They are only a manifest effect of actions by their elders. That's what terrifies Me."

"If they keep on, they will destroy the world," said St. Peter.

"Not the world. Just the earth. I created the Universe, you know. And I hate like Satan to start re-creating any part of it. But I appreciate your trying to appease My Wrath. And in keeping with My renowned Compassion, I will permit your Birthday celebration this year. But I warn you, next year I will be unmoved."

"By that time," replied St. Peter, "I hope those young men will have got rid of that long hair and those beards and the sandals and their robes . . ."

"Will you stop repeating that! Listen, I have a Son . . ."